SERIAL

KILLERS

OF

SANTA CRUZ

SERIAL KILLERS

OF SANTA CRUZ

AUBREY GRAVES

Disclaimer:

All references to copyrighted material are for
educational and informational purposes only
under the Fair Use Doctrine. U.S. Code: Title
17, § 107.

Table of Contents

San Francisco Examiner, September 29, 1974

Introduction

"MURDER CAPITAL OF THE WORLD"

In the 1970s, Santa Cruz County, California was home to a few extremely sick and evil psychotic killers. After the once-safe beach town endured a string of 27 murders over a span of 30 months, it became known as the alleged "Murder Capital of the World."

During this time, several bodies were found in the mountains, human remains washing up on shores, and some found lying on the side of the road. "Everywhere in Santa Cruz, people looked a little more closely at their neighbors. The person responsible for this butchery must be living a very bizarre double life, they thought. Where could someone so thoroughly mutilate and dismember those young women without being seen? How could one be so sick as to even contemplate such crimes without giving some hint of dangerous instability to family, friends or neighbors?" -Hugh Stephens, Inside Detective magazine, 1973.

The brutal killings started in 1970 with the tragic slaughter of the Ohta family and their friend by local mass murderer John Linley Frazier. Murders continued in 1972 and 1973, by Herbert Mullin and Edmund Kemper until these Santa Cruz serial killers were arrested. But it didn't stop there. In the 1980's, the Trailside Killer, David Carpenter, and Terry Childs, as well as several others terrorized the county, keeping the "murder capital" title alive.

Clip from the famous motion picture, The Lost Boys, 1989

SANTA CRUZ COUNTY

Is It Murder Capital?

FELTON (UPI) —The latest in a string of murders, four youths found shot to death in a tiny thatched cabin of the secluded Garden of Eden, had just wanted to live "away from it all," the brother of one victim said Sunday.

The youths were killed by a small caliber weapon investigators said. The slayings brought to 13 the number of known murders in Santa Cruz County since Jan. 9.

An autopsy was planned today.

Sheriff's deputies cordoned off the dirt trail leading to the small but sturdy cabin built under the shadows of an Oak Grove in the rugged Santa Cruz Mountains and said a massive "leaf by leaf" foot search of the area would continue today.

"We must be the murder capital of the world now," said Peter Chang, Santa Cruz County district attorney.

Jeffrey D. Card, 22, discovered the body of his brother, Brian, 20, and the three unidentified victims Saturday (Continued on Back Page)

ASST. SHERIFF LEE DAVIS LOOKS AT EVIDENCE
It Was Found With Bodies Of Four Youths

The Press Democrat, February 19, 1973

Killers: Santa Cruz in the '70s was home to four notorious murderers

Santa Cruz Sentinel, March 13, 2005

The 'Murder Capital' Title Has Stuck With Santa Cruz

MURDER BY NUMBERS

2 Decapitated

The serial killers of Santa Cruz

A time of terror

Murder Capital of the World

Why Santa Cruz?

Why did serial killers suddenly appear in Santa Cruz during the dozen years around the '70s?

Murder Rate Keeps Climbing

Santa Cruz County -- Murder Capital of World

The Press Democrat, February 1, 1973

UCSC Coed Found Slain In Cowell Park

Henry Cowell Park: of blossoms and bodies

murderous violence and a dumping ground for bodies the past two decades.

The history of the park's dark side is long and unfortunate.

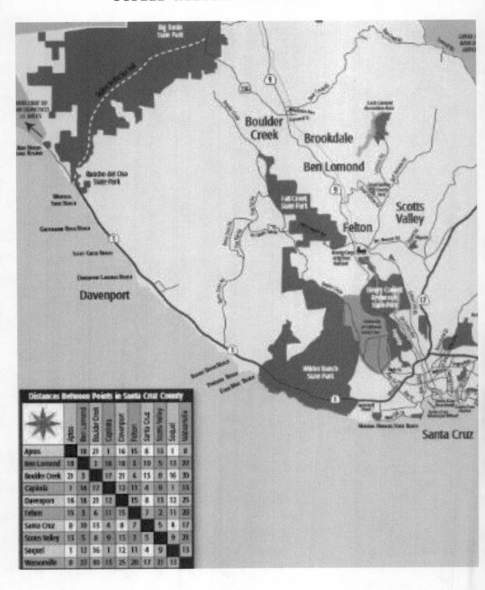

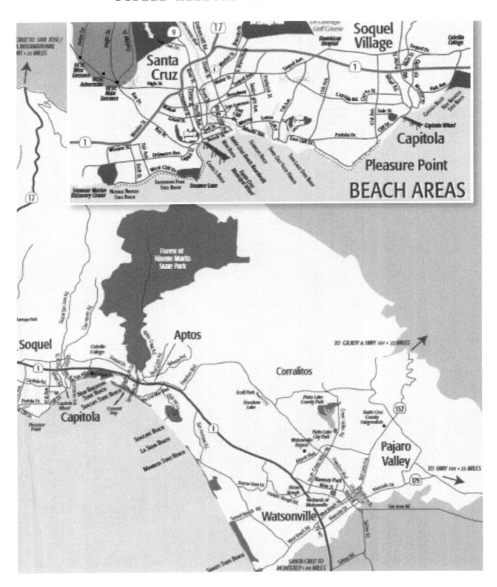

John Linley Frazier

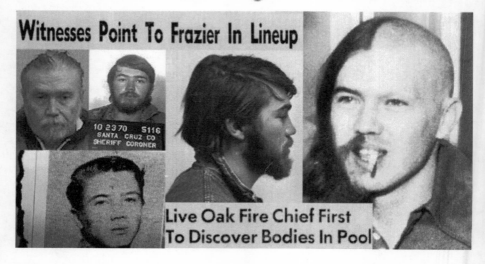

Witnesses Point To Frazier In Lineup

Live Oak Fire Chief First
To Discover Bodies In Pool

"Materialism must die or mankind will."

JOHN LINLEY FRAZIER

"The Killer Prophet"

Santa Cruz Mass Murderer

- <u>Date of birth</u>: January 26, 1946
- <u>Place of birth</u>: Hayward, Ohio
- <u>Date of death</u>: August 13, 2009 (aged 63)
- <u>Place of death</u>: Mule Creek State Prison, Ione, California
- <u>Cause of death</u>: Suicide by hanging
- <u>Conviction(s)</u>: First and second-degree Murder
- <u>Victims</u>: 5
- <u>Date of killings</u>: October 19, 1970
- <u>Date apprehended</u>: October 23, 1970
- <u>Criminal penalty</u>: Life imprisonment
- <u>Former residence</u>: Santa Cruz, California

15

Mass murderer John Linley Frazier was born on January 26, 1946 in Hayward, Ohio. Frazier had an unstable life from the start. In 1948, when he was two years old, his parents separated. A few years later in 1951, when he was five, his mother placed him in a foster home, unable to care for him.

Frazier attended Capitola School, in Capitola, a small city within Santa Cruz County. There, some classmates knew him as a "troublemaker."

John Linley Frazier as a boy, 1950's

His local eighth grade teacher remembers that "he didn't seem happy about the academic part of school. He was kind of a tuff kid. His attitude was poor at times.

He played football but didn't put himself out there much, or might have been good at sports."

John Frazier second from left in front row, eighth grade football team photo, Capitola School, Capitola, California

17

Frazier attended Santa Cruz High for only the first few weeks of his freshman year before dropping out of school completely.

Mug shot of Frazier as a juvenile, 1962

In 1962, when John Frazier was sixteen, he was arrested for burglary. He was placed in juvenile hall, where he escaped soon after.

He stayed out of trouble for a while after he began working as an auto mechanic and service attendant at various gas stations and shops around Santa Cruz, where he got along with most of his co-workers, and "most of the people that he worked with liked him." Though, his final employer shared that Frazier "flipped out" in the end, and also added that, "He was always a little unstable. He would easily become defensive when constructively criticized in his work."

In 1965, John Linley Frazier and his girlfriend Dolores had a child; two years later they were married. They lived in Felton, California, located in the Santa Cruz Mountains with several cats and dogs before he decided to go off the deep end.

In 1969, his wife noticed that he started having delusions. He would go off into the woods and take his bible and sometimes wouldn't come home for two or three days at a time. He began showing signs of schizophrenia, in addition to using a lot of hallucinogenic drugs. He then quit his job, moved out of his home, grew out his hair, and became an eco-freak.

After quitting his final job at twenty-four years of age, Frazier sold his tools and vowed never to ride in a car again because they pollute the environment. "He said God had told him that by driving his car he was polluting the environment and he would be killed if he drove anymore," said one acquaintance. And they weren't kidding. After he supposedly began receiving messages from the almighty, the acid-eating environmentalist truly believed that he was a prophet from God. He would rant and rave about how all materialists are hurting the environment and must be stopped. Frazier had also convinced himself that he was the John referred to in the New Testament's Book of Revelations, and was sent here by God to save the planet by restoring it to its natural state, which entailed removing all vehicles and buildings. His job under God's instruction was to give each head of household the option of choosing God's army or death. Frazier said that he was going to go door like the Avon lady and say, "Ding-dong, you're dead."

He saw his wife and mother's desperate attempts to get him to seek therapy as a conspiracy against him and his mission. Wanting more solitude, in July of 1970, he moved into a small, run-down storage shack on a property where his mother kept her trailer - off Cornwell Road in the Soquel Hills, in Santa Cruz County.

Frazier's shack, Santa Cruz, 1970

The Ohtas, a sweet, wealthy family lived across a large ravine from Frazier in their beautiful mansion at 999 North Rodeo Gulch Road, living happily and unaware that they would soon fall victim to their sick, delusional neighbor.

John Frazier began spying on the family, who he felt was very materialistic; he thought that their house was too big, and they had too many cars, and too much stuff. He ranted about it, saying, "people like that should be snuffed."

He even made a rickety old bridge that connected from their property to his. One afternoon while the family was out, he broke into the home and stole a pair of their binoculars, which he then used to watch them more closely.

Husband and father, Dr. Victor Ohta was a prominent eye surgeon in Santa Cruz where he had his own practice on Water Street. The wealthy forty-five-year-old and his wife, Virginia, had four children, two girls and two boys, in that order.

Virginia, Taggart (11), Derek (12) and Victor Ohta, circa 1970

The Ohta's daughters, Taura (18), and Lark (15), 1970

The Ohta's former residence, Soquel foothills, Santa Cruz, California, 1970

Frazier began to obsess over the family and would rant to some of his hiking buddies about the Ohtas, and even confessed to burglarizing the place.

Then, one day Frazier stopped by his wife's home in Felton and told her he was going to New York. He carried a loaded pistol and a backpack filled with food. Just before he left, he handed his estranged wife his deck of Tarot cards, his wallet, and driver's license. "I won't be needing these anymore," he told her.

The next night on October 19, 1970, Frazier committed one of the sickest and most tragic crimes in Santa Cruz history. He decided to go back to the Ohta house where he surprised Virginia Ohta (43), and youngest son, Taggart (11) inside the residence. Holding a .38 revolver on them, he tied their wrists and blindfolded them with a couple of the doctor's silk scarves.

Soon after, thirty-eight-year-old Dorothy Cadwallader, Victor's secretary and family friend, showed up with the Ohta's eldest son, Derek (12), whom she was dropping off. As each showed up, they were tied at gunpoint.

Dorothy Cadwallader, Dr. Ohta's secretary

Dr. Ohta returned home to find his family and secretary bound and terrified in their living room. Frazier tied Victor Ohta's hands behind his back while explaining to him what he had been instructed to do by God. He began to lecture the horrified captives about the evils of materialistic society and the ways in which it destroyed the environment.

He made Victor Ohta go outside by the pool and demanded that he burn down his house. Instead, Ohta offered him whatever he wanted, which made Frazier go completely berserk. He shoved Ohta into the pool, and as the doctor tried to get out of the water, Frazier grabbed a leaf skimmer and began to try and hold Dr. Ohta's head underneath the water with it. Every time he came up for air, Frazier would try and convince him to join God's army and burn down the house. When John thought he had finally convinced the doctor to join him, he held out his hand to help the doctor out of the pool, but Ohta had tricked him, pulling him into the water. Frazier, still holding the gun, shot Dr. Ohta three times, killing him in his pool.

The psychopath then had each of his victims come outside one at a time where he shot them in the back of the head execution style, one by one. Virginia, then Dorothy, then the boys, Derek, and Taggart, as well as the family cat. Luckily, the Ohta's daughters, Taura and Lark were away at boarding school. Frazier was reluctant to kill the children and began arguing with God saying that they are innocent and haven't done anything wrong, but he said that God insisted that they must die.

He threw all of his victims' bodies in the pool before typing a note on the Ohta's typewriter, setting the house ablaze, and stealing Virginia's car.

When the police arrived after spotting the fire, the driveway was blocked by the Ohta's vehicles. Fire Chief Ted Pound went around to the backyard to try and tap the home's swimming pool as a source of water to fight the growing blaze. He shined his flashlight on the pool to find a body floating on top of the water. As he looked down, he saw four more bodies on the bottom of the pool.

There were no weapons, no suspects, and no motive. All the detectives had was a typewritten note left on the windshield of one of the doctor's cars which read:

Halloween, 1970

Today World War III will begin as brought to you by The People of the Free Universe. From this day forward, anyone or company of persons who misuses the natural environment or destroys same will suffer the penalty of death by The People of the Free Universe. I and my comrades from this day forth will fight until death or freedom against any single anyone who does not support natural life on this planet, Materialism must die or mankind will.

-Knight of Wands, Knight of Cups, Night of Pentacles, and Knight of Swords

The ritualistic nature of the slayings, the cult-like tone of the note, and the signature of tarot card characters sparked terror in the community that another Manson family was in town on a bloody rampage.

Santa Cruz residents were beyond frightened. Everyone's doors were locked and guns were loaded.

'Most Tragic Murder'

Santa Cruz Sentinel, October 20, 1970

"The grisly murder of five people has set a fuse burning on long smoldering tensions in this Oceanside city."

WHERE FIVE WERE SLAIN — Map locates home of Dr. Victor M. Ohta who, with three members of his family and his secretary, was found slain Monday night.

The Sheboyga Press, October 20, 1970

—Associated Press WIREPHOTOS.

EXECUTION SCENE—Aerial photograph shows Dr. Victor Ohta's $250,-000 mansion, where his body, along with that of his wife and three others, was found yesterday in the swimming pool. The victims were shot in the back of the head, dumped into the pool, and then the mansion was set afire, presumably to call attention to the crime.

Press and Sun Bulletin, October 21, 1970

HOUSE OF DEATH

While firemen fought the fire at the palatial home of Dr. Victor Ohta near Santa Cruz last night, the body of the prominent eye surgeon, was found in the swimming pool along with the bodies of his wife, two children and his secretary. (AP Wirephoto)

Stevens Point Journal, October 20, 1970

31

The next day, Virginia Ohta's car was found inside the Rincon tunnel of the Southern Pacific Railroad near Henry Cowell State Park in Santa Cruz. A slow-moving switch engine had smashed into it around 4:45pm.

AP Wirephoto

FUGITIVE CAR—This is the car stolen from the death house of Dr. Victor Ohta. The occupants of the vehicle had left it on the tracks and were preparing to set it afire when the train came along.

The News Journal, October 21, 1970

32

Frazier's hiking buddies heard about the tragedy on the news and knew that he was responsible; he had just shared his People of the Free Universe letter with them a couple days prior. The three went to former District Attorney Peter Chang and shared with him everything they knew. Four days after the mass murder, John Linley Frazier was arrested at his shack.

John Linley Frazier, Santa Cruz County Jail, 1970

Frazier admitted to the murders, but pleaded not guilty by reason of insanity. His trial began in 1971, where he appeared to be barely in touch with reality.

There was more than enough physical evidence tying Frazier to the crime scene. Besides leaving his fingerprints in the stolen car, and on a beer can he left at the residence, they had an expert testify that a metallic substance found on Frazier's knife was consistent with the wire cords that had been cut inside the Ohta home.

Frazier was convicted of five accounts of murder in the first degree and was sentenced to die in San Quentin's gas chamber. A few years later his sentence was changed to life imprisonment due to California abolishing the death penalty in the early 70's.

About two years after the mass murder, unable to come to terms with it all, Dr. Ohta's mother committed suicide.

In 1977, almost seven years after the tragedy, the eldest daughter, Taura (25) also took her life as she wasn't able to bare the death of her family and friend. She was laid to rest next to her family at the Holy Cross Cemetery in Santa Cruz.

About 30 years later in November 2008, when John Linley Frazier was once again up for parole, Santa Cruz Assistant District Attorney issued a statement, "Some people deserve to be punished for the rest of their lives. Frazier is such a man."

Nine months later, on August 13, 2009, the killer hung himself in his prison cell in Mule Creek State Prison, in Ione, California.

"A correctional officer found Frazier, 62, unresponsive in his cell on August 13th. He was pronounced dead at 1:33 p.m., prison officials reported. He died of asphyxiation and the Amador County coroner ruled it was a suicide, said Amador County Undersheriff James Wegner. 'It was a hanging,' Wegner said. Frazier was in his cell alone. Mule Creek State Prison spokeswoman Terry Thorton did not know the last time he had been checked on." -San Jose Mercury News, 2009

In 2013, youngest daughter and only survivor, Lark Ohta, spoke on a television series called *Born to Kill?*, and shared her heart-breaking experience of how she found out her family had been tragically murdered.

"I was back at boarding school and I was woken up by one of the nuns and told that I needed to go home. And it certainly was not anything I could have imagined. When I walked outside it was just barley sunrise and all the nuns from the entire school were standing outside. They had to tell me in the car that my family had died. It was unthinkable."

The Ohta Family Is 'With Christ'

Santa Cruz Sentinel, October 23, 1970

Dr Victor Masashi Ohta — Virginia Ann Ohta — Derek Richard Ohta — Taggart Victor Ohta — Dorothy Cadwallader

The Ohta Family and Dr Ohta's Secretary

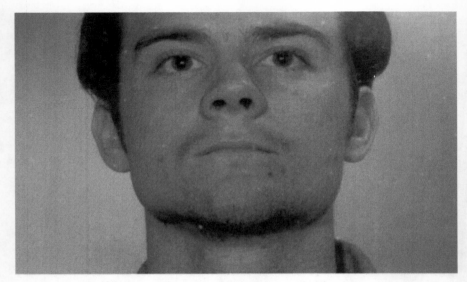

Herbert Mullin

"Satan gets into us and makes us do things that we don't want to do."

HERBERT WILLIAM MULLIN

Santa Cruz Serial Killer

- <u>Date of birth</u>: April 18, 1947
- <u>Place of birth</u>: Salinas, California
- <u>Height</u>: 5 ft, 7 in
- <u>Conviction(s)</u>: First and second-degree murder
- <u>Victims</u>: 13
- <u>Span of killings</u>: October 13, 1972 - February 13, 1973
- <u>Date apprehended</u>: February 13, 1973
- <u>Criminal penalty</u>: Life imprisonment
- <u>Former residence</u>: Felton, California
- <u>Incarcerated at</u>: Mule Creek State Prison, Ione, California

The delusional, paranoid schizophrenic, Herbert Mullin, was convicted of killing thirteen people, and charged with killing ten of them after his killing-spree in 1972 and 1973. The majority of his innocent victims were Santa Cruz county residents.

Born in Salinas, California on April 18, 1947, Herbert Mullin was raised in a strict Catholic household with his older sister Patricia in a farming area just south of San Francisco, California. His father, Bill Mullin was a furniture salesman, and his mother, Jean Mullin, was an "overly religious" housewife.

Herbert was said to be a "gentle natured child" and very bright. In addition to being a Boy Scout, and an altar boy when he was young, Mullin was also on a little league team for several years.

In 1963, when he was sixteen, he and his parents moved to the small, quiet town of Felton, California, located deep in the Santa Cruz Mountains.

His first two years of high school were spent at an all-boys catholic school. His parents transferred him to San Lorenzo Valley High School in Felton his junior year, where he was a well-liked, popular football player, and honor student.

Herbert Mullin's yearbook photo, junior year, San Lorenzo Valley High, Felton, CA, 1964

Mullin also played basketball and baseball, and was vice president of the Varsity Club during his senior year. He even had a high school sweetheart named Loretta Ricketts- whom he dated for several years.

Herbert Mullin (number 72), San Lorenzo Valley High School Varsity Football photo, Felton, 1965

Herbert Mullin, senior year, 1965

In 1965, Herb graduated from San Lorenzo Valley High School at the top of his class. He was voted "most likely to succeed" by his classmates in their high school yearbook.

The summer after graduation, Herb's best friend, Dean Richardson, was killed in a car accident. Mullin took it very hard and was never the same again. His friend's untimely end triggered his schizophrenia and insanity.

In 1966, Herb began studying civil highway technology at Cabrillo College, located in Aptos (in Santa Cruz County).

During this time he broke up with his high school sweetheart, Loretta, before getting back together, and getting engaged in 1967.

In his sophomore year of college, Herb began experimenting with LSD, escalating his mental illness. His friends and family began to notice that he wasn't the same guy he was in high school; there was something just not right about him.

After graduating with a B average from Cabrillo College, he moved into a boardinghouse in San Jose, California, where he attended San Jose State and became a dish washer at a nearby restaurant.

Mullin began to feel attracted to men and was worried that he was going to go to hell for having homosexual urges. So he dropped out of college and devoted all of his time to the study of Hinduism and yoga, in hope that his faith and dedication would make up for his sins.

In January of 1968, he had sex with a man and accepted himself as bisexual. A few months later in April of 1968, he broke off his engagement with Loretta, and they were done for good.

That summer, he moved to San Luis Obispo, California where he managed a thrift store and rented an apartment.

In February of 1969, Mullin moved back to his family's Felton home claiming that he was going to move to India to study religion. A few weeks later, he checked into the Mendocino State Hospital, in Mendocino, California. Psychiatrists diagnosed him with severe paranoid schizophrenia and put him on antipsychotics. While at the hospital, he admitted to hearing voices telling him what to do; he "listened to cosmic emanations for guidance."

In May, he was released from the mental facility, insisting that he was better. Unfortunately due to the fact that Herb was a voluntary patient, the hospital was unable to hold him there against his will.

In late October, Mullin drove down to San Luis Obispo to visit some old friends. One was his former boss; he shared with him that he began hearing voices telling him to do things, and some of these things he did, such as burning his penis with lit cigarettes.

One of his other friends was concerned with Mullin's behavior, and he called authorities who then committed Mullin to the San Luis Obispo General Hospital on Halloween of 1969. Three days later he was back out on the streets.

He headed south, and about a day later he was picked up by the police after they received a report that he was arguing with himself and exposing his penis to people as they walked by. He was 5150ed once again, with a file that read: "as a result of a mental disorder he is a danger to others, a danger to himself, and gravely disabled."

After pressuring the psychiatrists and doctors for his release, he was able to go home a couple weeks later, as long as he'd become an out-patient at the Santa Cruz Mental Health Clinic. Mullin visited the clinic for about seven months but never kept up on his daily medication.

He became a bus-boy at the Holiday Inn on Ocean Street in Santa Cruz, and moved into a cheap hotel (claimed to be where the Sunshine Villa is currently) near the main beach.

During that time, Herbert Mullin met a woman at a local commune that was said to be almost crazier than him, with the mentality of a child. They instantly "fell-in-love" and became "soul mates" overnight. She convinced him to run away with her to Hawaii, and when they did, she abandoned him the very next day in Maui. The following day, Mullin decided to check himself into the island's mental facility for therapy. He was discharged about three weeks later.

Two days after his release, he was arrested for possession and for being under the influence. During his hearing, he yelled at the Santa Cruz judge, demanding that Marijuana and LSD be legalized. The judge committed him to the local emergency mental ward, where he was held for 72 hours.

Mullin constantly moved to different places and in and out of his parent's house.

He began getting into yelling matches with God, terrifying his roommate in San Francisco, California, where he lived for a short amount of time in 1971.

While living up in the city, Herbert Mullin began thinking about his birthday, and finding it extremely significant that he was born on the anniversary of the 1906 San Francisco Earthquake, as well as the anniversary of Albert Einstein's death. Both of these events in Mullin's twisted mind gave him the cosmic duty to kill.

"By September of 1972, Herb KNEW that reincarnation worked both forward and backward in time, that he not only could be born again in the future, but also in the past. It had become obvious to him that Einstein had died to protect him and all beings born on April 18ᵗʰ from dying in the great disaster of his generation, -the Vietnam war. Now Herb must make a sacrifice to prevent a repeat of the earthquake that had occurred on his birthday, which was predicted a few months hence. He considered suicide, but one life would not be enough. To prevent so great cataclysm would

require a bigger commitment, both to avert it and guarantee his birth position in the next (or past) life." - "The Die Song", Donald Lunde and Jefferson Morgan, 1980.

> *"It was time to sing the die song."*
>
> -Herbert Mullin

Mullin's parents were seeking a mental hospital where he could be committed permanently. Unfortunately, many hospitals had closed and the few that were open were too expensive. So the family could do nothing but pray that Herbert wouldn't hurt anyone.

About a month before the murders, at twenty-five years of age, Mullin moved back in with his parents at their Felton home located at 1541 McLellan Road.

While there, Mullin tried to fight his dad saying, "Come on, let's go, it won't last long," before punching him out. "It scared me," his father, Martin Mullin stated. "It was such a departure from what we had normally done all our lives - he was not the same kid we had raised and known."

A few weeks later, around noon on October 13th, 1972, Mullin spotted his first victim, a fifty-five-year-old local transient by the name of Lawrence White (Whitey) who was walking alone along Highway 9 in the Santa Cruz mountains. Mullin drove by Whitey, and immediately pulled over, pretending to have car trouble. When Whitey stopped and offered to help, Mullin beat him to death with a baseball bat, pushing his lifeless body off the side of the highway.

Lawrence White, Mullin's first victim

Mullin later claimed that victim Lawrence White was Jonah from the Bible, and that he had sent him a telepathic message saying, "Pick me up and throw me over the boat. Kill me so that others will be saved."

Lawrence White was buried at Oakwood Cemetery in Santa Cruz on October 20th, 1972. Unfortunately no one attended his funeral.

> *"We human beings, through the history of the world, have prevented our continent from cataclysms by murder. In other words, a minor natural disaster avoids a major natural disaster."*
>
> -Herbert Mullin

Eleven days later, Mullin struck again. On October 24th, 1972, he picked up twenty-four-year-old student, Mary Guilfoyle, who was hitchhiking in front of Cabrillo College, in Aptos, California. Seeing that Mullin was a smaller, younger man, she felt he wasn't much of a threat, and got into his blue '58 Chevy station wagon without hesitation. The beautiful, 5'7", 115-pound bombshell in a little red dress explained she was late for an interview downtown and needed to get there as soon as possible.

Mullin's second victim, Mary Guilfoyle

Herb got on the freeway from Park Avenue and headed toward downtown Santa Cruz, but he got off the freeway an exit too soon, on Emeline, telling the young co-ed that it was a faster route. In a sudden swift move, he pulled the car over on the side of the road, took his hunting knife out from under his seat, and stabbed Mary Guilfoyle directly in the heart. The poor young woman died instantly and slumped forward. Mullin continued to stab her two more times in the back. He sat the knife next to her body and started his car back up.

He drove her corpse to Smith Grade Road (a rural road in Bonny Doon that's in the Santa Cruz Mountains), where he dragged her body out of the car, sliced her open, and pulled out her organs. Covered in her blood, Mullin got up and took one last look at her lifeless body staring back at him, before he got back in his car and drove home.

Feeling remorseful for his two cold-blooded murders, Mullin decided he needed to confess his sins. On November 2nd, 1972 (All Souls Day) he drove drunk to St. Mary's Catholic Church in Los Gatos, California (about 20 miles north of Santa Cruz) "to give {him} strength to never attempt to kill again."

Sixty-four-year-old Father Henri Tomei was in the confessional when Mullin entered the empty church.

Father Henri Tomei, Mullin's third victim

His plans of confession changed after he saw a light over the confessional booth and heard a voice say, "That's the person to kill." Mullin tried to open the door to the confession booth, but it was locked, so he began rattling the knob. The priest got up and unlocked and opened the door to see crazy Herb standing before him. Without any hesitation, he stabbed

Father Tomei in the chest, who then fell back into the booth. Fighting for his life, he kicked Mullin in the head and whispered, "Mon Dieu." Sadly, he stabbed the father three more times. As he wiped the blood off his knife, he heard a scream and retreating footsteps. He walked quickly out of the church, and got into his car, heading back over Highway 17 without anyone else seeing him.

The community was outraged by the sick and senseless murder of Father Tomei, who was a known hero in the French Resistance movement in World War II.

After his arrest, Herbert Mullin's mother was shocked to find out her son had murdered Father Tomei saying, "He'd been a deeply religious child, you know, altar boy in the Catholic Religion."

On December 16th, 1972, Mullin bought his first fire arm; a .22 caliber revolver at the late Western Auto store in Felton, California.

Around this time, he tried to join the Coast Guard but was denied because he failed the psychological exam, leaving him to believe that it was all a conspiracy against him. He blamed the hippies and war resistors since they brainwashed him by giving him drugs and talked him into being a pacifist.

He began having urges to kill once again, but this time he was going after the people who he believed ruined his life. "The peace advocates and flower children had played tricks on my mind, and I had to reap vengeance," stated Mullin in an interview after his arrest.

Herb decided to start with the man who introduced him to drugs, his old high school buddy, twenty-five year old Jim Gianera who sold him marijuana in the past.

On the morning of January 25th, 1973, he drove up to Gianera's last known residence on Mystery Spot Road in Santa Cruz. When Mullin arrived at the tiny run-down cabin, he was told by the new tenant, Kathy Francis, that Jim Gianera and his wife, Joan, moved to the west side of Santa Cruz. Kathy Francis, twenty-nine-year-old wife and mother of two, had the Gianera's present address and gave it to Mullin unaware that she just gave him his ticket for a completely tragic and horrific murder spree.

Mullin drove straight to Jim and Joan Gianera's house at 1520 Western Drive. Twenty-one-year-old Joan was upstairs taking a shower when Jim answered the door. As soon as Herbert Mullin entered the home, he pulled out his gun and shot Jim in the arm. Jim ran into the kitchen and opened the fridge door, hiding behind it and using it as a shield, grasping for a weapon, but Mullin shot him again, this time in the elbow, shattering the bone. Jim charged at Herbert who continued firing, shooting Jim in the ribcage, puncturing his lung. Jim scrambled up the staircase to get to Joan, who had just gotten out of the shower. As he got to the top of the staircase, Mullin shot him one last time in the head. At that moment, Joan opened the door to see her beloved husband on his knees, covered in blood. She looked up to see Mullin standing behind him pointing a gun at her. Before she could react, Mullin shot her in the chest; she fell to the ground next to Jim, who was taking his final breaths. "I love you," she told him. Mullin took out his hunting knife and viscously stabbed Joan twice in the back, before shooting her three more times in the neck.

The couple's bodies were discovered late that morning by Joan's mother, who was returning their infant daughter from a sleepover the night before.

2—Santa Cruz Sentinel   Friday, Jan. 26, 1973

Pair Found Dead

This is the house at 1520 Western Drive in   of James Ralph Gianera, 24, and his wife,
which city police this morning found the bodies   Joan, 21.

Santa Cruz Sentinel, January 26, 1973

As soon as Mullin left their home, he began to worry that he would be ratted out to authorities by Kathy Francis for asking for the Gianera's address. Mullin went right back to the Francis residence to do what he felt had to be done. Kathy's husband was away on business, and so she was home alone with her boys, nine-year-old David Hughes, and four-year-old Daemon Francis.

Victims Kathy Francis, and her two boys, David Hughes (left), and Daemon Francis (right)

Herb burst into the cold, dark home to find Kathy standing at the kitchen counter. Holding his gun in plain sight, he asked Kathy if he could have a few words with her. Without letting her answer, he shot her in the chest, and again in her head. He then went into the boys' room and shot them both while they were on their bunk bed playing Chinese checkers. He took out his hunting knife and stabbed each of the boys once in the back, before returning to Kathy and stabbing her once in her chest; then he quickly left the residence.

A neighbor saw Mullin leave the Francis home, but wasn't able to give a good description of what he or his vehicle looked like. Mullin got away with it all, once again.

Santa Cruz Sentinel, January 26, 1973

Francis residence crime scene photos, Santa Cruz, CA. Bottom left: Kathy Francis deceased, January 25, 1973

Mullin's victim, Kathy Francis dead in her home, Mystery Spot Road, Santa Cruz, CA

On February 10th, 1973, at Henry Cowell Redwoods State Park, in an area of Santa Cruz called "Inspiration Point," Mullin came across four teenage boys who were illegally camping in a makeshift tent made out of tarps and wood. Having lived there for several months, on this night, the boys were sitting down to for a macaroni and cheese dinner when Mullin confronted them.   He   told   them   they   were defacing state property and demanded that they pack up and leave. Mullin had once been hassled by a park ranger who told him the same thing, so he found it unfair that the boys were doing it and getting away with it; he became enraged. Laughing at Mullin for trying to have some kind of authority, the boys refused to leave, setting the psycho killer off the rails. Mullin pulled out his gun and began shooting. Robert Spector (18), David Olicker (18), Brian Scott Card (19), and Mark Dreibelbis (15) were all killed instantly.

From left to right: Robert Spector, David Olicker, and Mark Dreibelbis. (Brian Scott Card not shown.)

Before leaving the horrific scene, Mullin stole a rifle and twenty dollars.

The boys were found a few days later by victim Brain Card's older brother who contacted authorities.

"We must be the murder capital of the world right now," said Santa Cruz District Attorney Peter Chang. That very quote is what gave Santa Cruz the title, which has never been forgotten.

Crime scene photo, Henry Cowell Redwoods State Park, Santa Cruz, CA, 1973

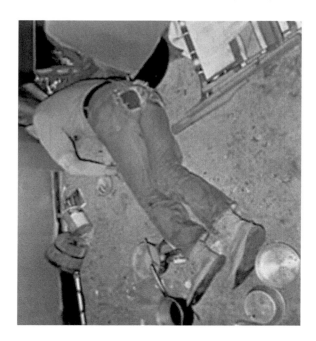

Crime scene photos, Henry Cowell Redwoods State Park, Santa Cruz, CA, 1973

Crime scene photo of men carrying one of Mullin's victims in a body bag, Henry Cowell Redwoods State Park, Santa Cruz, 1973

Santa Cruz Murder Victims · Wanted To Live In The Wilds

Daily Independent Journal, February 19, 1973

FELTON, Calif. (UPI) — The latest in a string of murders, four youths found shot to death in a tiny thatched cabin of the secluded Garden of Eden, had just wanted to live "away from it all," the brother of one victim said Sunday.

The youths were killed by a small caliber weapon investigators said. The slayings brought to 13 the number of known murders in Santa Cruz County since Jan. 9.

Daily Independent Journal, February 19, 1973

Three days later, on the morning of February 13th, Mullin's parents asked him to go pick up some firewood. While on the errand, Herbert heard his father's voice say to him, "Before you deliver the wood, I want you to kill me somebody." Driving through the west side of Santa Cruz seeking his thirteenth victim, he came across an elderly man weeding his lawn at 511 Lighthouse Avenue. Herb pulled over and shot seventy-two-year-old local Fred Perez with the rifle he had pilfered from his last victims' campsite. He then drove off "calmly," as stated by eye witnesses who gave this information to the police; they caught him just a few minutes later. Mullin was arrested on ten counts of murder at the intersection of Highway 9 and Coral Street in Santa Cruz. The murder spree was finally over.

Herbert Mullin during trial, 1973

Mullin Arrested on 10 Charges of Murder

SANTA CRUZ, Calif. (AP) — Herbert Mullin, a former honors student, was arraigned here yesterday on charges of murdering 10 perdsons.

Judge Charles Franich gave Mullin until March 27 to enter a plea of guilty or innocent after reading the grand jury transcript of his indictment preceedings.

The son of a retired Marine officer, Mullin is accused of killing a woman and her two children in a cabin Jan. 15, a young couple the same day, four young campers two weeks later and a 72-year-old ex-prizefighter.

During the arraignment F r a n i c h amended a gag rule and ordered grand jurors as well as police officers not to comment on the case.

The judge also ordered the grand jury transcript sealed for at least 10 days after Mullin receives a copy of it.

Mullin, 25, has been held without bail in the San Mateo county jail. A request from Mullin's attorney that his client be moved to the Santa Cruz county jail was dismissed because of inadequate facilities there.

AP wirephoto

Herbert Mullin

. . . 10 murder charges

The San Bernardino County, March 17, 1973

During questioning, Herbert Mullin repeatedly said, "Silence!" claiming that his father, war veteran Martin William Mullin, was also the reason for the murders. He said that

69

his father had telepathically commanded him to murder people, saying, "Why won't you give me anything?! Go kill somebody! Move!"

Throughout the years following his arrest, Mullin was caught in a spiraling pattern of rebellion and reconciliation with his dad. One psychiatrist, in his testimony for the prosecution, said that Mullin's "inability to express hate to his father led to some of it being misdirected to others."

While awaiting trial, Mullin stayed at the former Santa Cruz County Jail with Ed Kemper. With adjacent cells, Kemper was known to both bully Mullin and keep him in check. "Well, he had a habit of singing and bothering people when somebody tried to watch TV, so I threw water on him to shut him up," Kemper shared. "Then, when he was a good boy, I'd give him some peanuts. Herbie liked peanuts. That was effective, because pretty soon he asked permission to sing. That's called behavior modification treatment," Kemper stated.

During the trial, Mullin said that he ignored messages to kill. "I received a message in December I did not act on. I just didn't want to kill anymore. I just didn't think it was right," Mullin said to the court. He was admitting he knew the difference between right and wrong, and was not his father's "robot," powerless to disobey, as he had previously stated.

Herbert Mullin during trial, 1973

In the end, Mullin was convicted of ten counts of murder in Santa Cruz County. He was found guilty of two counts of first degree murder for the killings of James Gianera and Kathy Francis, and eight counts of second degree murder, because the jury found his "diminished capacity" limited his ability to premeditate. He was never charged with the murder of Mary Guilfoyle and Lawrence White, though he admitted to them. A Santa Clara County jury convicted him of Father Henri Tomei's murder.

The cold-blooded killer remains behind bars (hopefully for the rest of his life) at Mule Creek State Prison, in Ione, California.

"I believe that my father has been unequally blamed for my failures. But surely, if he had given me the six-year old homosexual "blow job" oral stimulation that I was entitled to, like most other people get, I would never had taken LSD without his permission."

-Herbert Mullin

"*I wish that I had run into someone that could have straightened out my life, so I would not have taken those people's lives. About four or five times, I had two choices to make and I would stand there and think about it, and then usually make the wrong choice.*"

— Herbert Mullin

Herbert Mullin, circa 2010

Herbert Mullin's victims (10 of 13)

Herbert Mullin's Victims

- Lawrence White, 55. October 13, 1972
- Mary Guilfoyle, 24. October 24, 1972
- Rev. Henri Tomei, 64. November 2, 1972
- James (Jim) Gianera, 25. January 25, 1973
- Joan Gianera, 21. January 25, 1973
- Kathleen Francis, 29. January 25, 1973
- David Hughes, 9. January 25, 1973
- Daemon Francis, 4. January 25, 1973
- Robert Spector, 18. February 10, 1973
- David Oliker, 18. February 10, 1973
- Brian Scott Card, 19. February 10, 1973
- Mark Dreibelbis, 15. February 10, 1973
- Fred Perez, 72. February 13, 1973

May you all rest in peace.

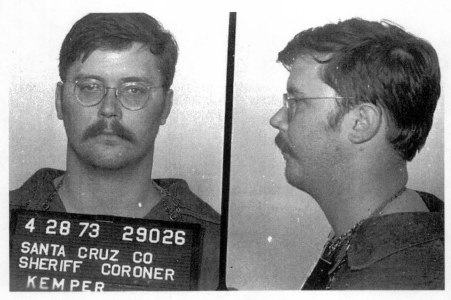

Edmund Kemper

Kemper Guilty

"The Co-Ed Killer"

2—Santa Cruz Sentinel Sunday, April 29, 1973

**Kemper Leads Lawmen
To Several Burial Sites**

"When I see a pretty girl walking down the street, I think two things. One part wants to be real nice and sweet. And the other part wonders what her head would look like on a stick."

EDMUND EMIL KEMPER III

"The Co-Ed Killer," "The Co-Ed Butcher"

Psychopathic serial killer, necrophiliac from Santa Cruz, California

- <u>Date of birth</u>: December 18, 1948
- <u>Place of birth</u>: Burbank, California
- <u>Height</u>: 6 ft, 9 in
- <u>Conviction(s)</u>: First-degree murder
- <u>Victims</u>: 10
- <u>Span of killings</u>: August 27, 1964 - April 20, 1973
- <u>Date apprehended</u>: April 21, 1973
- <u>Criminal penalty</u>: Life imprisonment
- <u>Former residence</u>: Aptos, California
- <u>Incarcerated at</u>: California Medical Facility, Vacaville, CA

One of the sickest people to ever walk the earth is the notorious Santa Cruz serial killer, Edmund Emil Kemper III. Born on December 18th, 1948, in Burbank, California, the left-handed "co-ed killer" with a very high IQ of 136, had disturbing behavior from the very beginning. He was obsessed with death since he was a young boy, whose favorite games to play were "the gas chamber" and "the electric chair." He loved ripping the heads off his sisters' dolls and would pretend it was their mother, Clarnell, who was extremely physically and verbally abusive.

Clarnell Strandberg, Ed Kemper's mother

Ed's sister used to tease him about having a crush on his elementary school teacher, saying that he wanted to kiss her. He replied that if he kissed her, he'd have to kill her first.

It got much worse after his parents divorced in 1957; he had to move with his mother and two older sisters to Helena, Montana. His mother, who had borderline personality disorder, began locking him in the basement at night for fear he would molest his sisters in their sleep.

Getting fed up with the constant abuse, Kemper once went into a cathedral and prayed that everyone in the world would die except him. He began to fantasize about killing people, sometimes in groups.

At the age of ten, he killed their family cat by burying it alive. He then dug it up, dismembered it, and even went to the extent of putting its poor head on a stick.

At thirteen years of age, Kemper killed another one of their cats because the cat showed more affection to his sister. In a jealous rage, he cut the cat up into pieces and then kept part of its corpse in his closet.

At the age of fifteen, having a hard time getting along with his mother, Kemper went to live with his father in Van Nuys, California. His father had already remarried and had another son; this made Kemper jealous, and resentful. Unhappy with his father, he would fantasize that Hollywood actor, John Wayne was his dad.

Soon after Edmund had moved in with his father, he was sent to live with his grandparents in North Fork, California. His father was just unable to cope with his behavior.

Kemper moved in with his grandparents Edmund and Maude on their 17-acre farm during the holidays of 1963. He began attending Sierra Joint Union High School in nearby Tollhouse, California, where he made good grades and wasn't a bother to anyone. His grandfather gave him a .22 caliber rifle with which he shot rabbits, gophers, birds, and other small animals.

When Kemper's mother heard that he moved in with his grandparents, she called his father to have him warn them, "That guy is a real weirdo and you're taking a chance leaving him with your parents. You might be surprised to wake up some morning and learn they have been killed." His father knew his son was weird, but he didn't think he was dangerous, so he just brushed off his ex-wife's concerns.

At the end of the school year, Kemper returned to Montana to stay with his mother for the summer, but ended up going back to the farm two weeks later. His grandmother noticed that Ed wasn't the same as soon as he arrived; he seemed even more sullen and ominous than usual. Ed could tell his grandmother no longer trusted him, and he found the lack of trust to be an insult. This started an abundant amount of tension and Kemper was getting more annoyed with her by the day. He began fantasizing about his grandmother standing in the outhouse as he shot it full of holes.

On August 27th, 1964, Kemper's dark fantasy basically became reality. While sitting at the kitchen table with grandmother, Maude, (who reminded him so much of his crazy mother), they began to get into a heated argument. Enraged, Ed stood up and said he was going hunting and grabbed his gun, whistled for his dog, and walked out the front door. He then turned around and through an open window he shot his 66-year-old grandmother in the back of the head. As she slumped on the table, he shot her two more times in the back. He pulled her into one of the bedrooms, got a butcher knife from the kitchen, and brutally stabbed her dead body three times.

Kemper's grandfather came home soon after the attack. While unloading his truck, Edmund shot his grandfather in the back of the head. He later said that he killed his 72-year-old grandfather, Edmund Kemper Sr., because he didn't want him to have to experience the death of his wife. Ed quickly dragged his grandfather's body into the garage and called his mother to confess. She urged him to call the police, so he did.

'Fire In The Cannon'; Couple Slain

'Granddad Smiling At Me...
...I Didn't Want Him To See'

Boy, 15 Says
He Killed Kin

1964

Edmund Kemper's mug shot, 1964

Wed., Sept. 23, 1964	THE DAILY SUN—A-7

Boy, 15, Sentenced to CYA For Slaying Grandparents

The Daily Sun, September 23, 1964

> *"I just wanted to see how it felt to shoot Grandma."*
>
> -Ed Kemper

After his arrest, Kemper was handed over to the California Youth Authority and was eventually sent to Atascadero State Hospital, a maximum security facility for mentally ill convicts in Atascadero, California. There, he became more obsessed with killing and sex - in that order. He constantly fantasized about killing young women and having sex with their corpses.

In 1969, at twenty-one years of age, Kemper somehow convinced the doctors he was well enough to be released from the mental hospital.

He then enrolled in community college in San Luis Obispo for a semester before he moved back in with his mother, Clarnell. She had recently moved back to California after her third divorce, taking a job as a secretary at the University in Santa Cruz. She rented a three bedroom duplex at 609-A Ord Street, in Aptos, California.

Kemper's residence (lower level) in Aptos, California

Their toxic relationship only escalated and they began getting into big, loud arguments, disturbing the neighbors. Clarnell continued to scold Kemper, so he often sought refuge at a local bar, The Jury Room. The 6'9" giant, who was known there as "Big Ed", became a regular at the Santa Cruz dive bar on Ocean Street. There, he oddly made friends with local police officers and deputies, who (obviously) had no idea what kind of person they had befriended.

The Jury Room, Kemper's old haunt, Santa Cruz, CA

Kemper had developed an interest in being a cop but was unable to meet the requirements due to his size.

In 1971 Kemper got a job with the Division of Highways, which enabled him to move out of his mother's home and into a room of an apartment in Alameda, California. He still couldn't get away from his nagging mother, who would pay him surprise visits and constantly call and bug him.

Kemper was on the prowl for a girlfriend - his very first girlfriend. He began dating a 17-year-old girl from Turlock, California whose name was never disclosed. They met on the beach in Santa Cruz and became engaged almost immediately.

He bought a motorcycle and about a year later he was in an accident breaking his arm. His work gave him time off to recuperate, and during that time, with the settlement from the car accident, he bought a yellow 1969 Ford Galaxie with a black roof top.

With too much time on his hands, Kemper began picking up hitchhikers (mainly young college girls) and fantasized about all the sick things he could do to them.

He even stuck one of his mother's UCSC staff stickers on the back of his car to make it look like he worked for the university, which would make hitchhikers feel more at ease.

After giving rides to about 150 travelers, he began to store and build his psycho-killer collection of knives, handcuffs, plastic bags, and blankets in the trunk of his car. His evil urges of murder and necrophilia grew by the day.

Shit got real on May 7th, 1972 when Kemper was driving through Berkeley, California and picked up two co-eds from Fresno State University that were hitchhiking. 19-year-old Mary Ann Pesce and her roommate, 18-year-old Anita Luchessa, were on their way to visit friends at Standford University in Palo Alto, California. Instead, Kemper drove them to a secluded wooded area of Alameda to meet their maker.

Victim, Mary Ann Pesce

Victim, Anita Luchessa

He handcuffed Mary Ann Pesce to the arm rest in the backseat, and ordered Anita Luchessa to get in the trunk of his car. He began smothering Pesce who fought for her life with all her might. As she bit through the bag he had put over her head, he began stabbing the young victim in the back, and finally slit her throat. He then forced Luchessa out of the trunk and stabbed her to death. He put their bodies in the trunk of his car and started heading home.

Almost to his apartment, he was pulled over for having a tail light out; he stayed calm and wasn't questioned or searched, so unfortunately he got away.

He arrived to his apartment in Alameda at 916 Union Street to find his roommate gone. He quickly carried the girls' lifeless bodies, wrapped in blankets, through the complex to his room. He undressed his victims and took photos of them as he had sexual intercourse with their corpses. He then decapitated them and performed irrumatio on their severed heads before dismembering them completely. After taking more photos, he placed their body parts in bags and buried them near the Santa Cruz summit in the Loma Prieta Mountains.

The deranged maniac kept the girls' heads in his closet and had sex with them until they decayed. He threw them into a ravine close to where their body parts laid in a shallow grave.

"It was the first time I went looking for someone to kill. And it's two people, not one. And they're dead. Very naïve, too. Painfully naïve in that they thought they were streetwise."

-Ed Kemper

Daily Independent Journal, July 1, 1972

Kemper: The 'murderous butcher'

A few months later, on August 15th, 1972, Mary Ann Pesce's skull was found by two target shooters.

Anita Luchessa's remains were never found.

About four months after he murdered the two co-eds, Kemper began having urges to kill again, which he called his "little zapples."

On the evening of September 14th, 1972, Ed picked up another victim in Berkeley, California. Aiko Koo was a beautiful and talented 15-year-old girl who was on her way to dance class, but had missed her bus. Running late, she began hitchhiking (after her mother specifically told her not to). Ed pulled over and offered her a ride.

While on the road, he pulled his gun out and Aiko became hysterical. To calm her down, he told her that he was going to use it to shoot himself, and that if she didn't try to signal police or passersby, she would not be harmed.

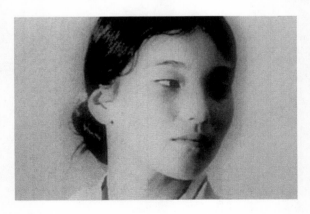

Aiko Koo, victim of Ed Kemper

They drove for over an hour to Bonny Doon, located deep in the Santa Cruz Mountains. He parked in a remote area, where he got out of the car, accidentally locking himself out. "She could have reached over and grabbed the gun," Kemper said later, "but I think she never gave it a thought." Instead, she unlocked the door and let the killer back in.

He covered the young girl's mouth and nose and suffocated her to death. He then took her out of the car, laid her on the ground, and raped her. Making sure she was dead, Kemper then strangled her with her scarf, and then began dissecting her.

He put her body parts in the trunk and drove into town, stopping at a local bar. There, he had a couple of beers before going by his mother's house.

Throughout the evening, he would open the trunk "admiring his catch like a fisherman."

Late that night he brought Aiko Koo's dismembered body back to his Alameda apartment, where he had sex with it again.

Two days after the tragic slaying of Aiko Koo, Kemper had a doctor's appointment where Fresno psychiatrists examined him; they found him "no longer a danger to society." While he was at his psychiatric appointment, Koo's head sat in the trunk of his car.

Kemper declared 'harmless' two days after girl killed

Progress Bulletin, May 1, 1973

He disposed of her head, hands, and the rest of her corpse separately around Alameda County, as well as in Boulder Creek (in the Santa Cruz Mountains).

> *"When someone put their hand on my car-door handle, they were giving me their life."*
>
> -Ed Kemper

In the winter of 1972, Kemper moved back in to his mother's duplex on Ord Street in Aptos, California. He began driving by Cabrillo

College, (just a few miles from their home) hunting for his next victim.

Then, on January 8th, 1973, the co-ed killer struck again. This time it was 19-year-old Cabrillo College student, Cynthia Schall, who was hitchhiking to class. He took the co-ed to a sequestered area in Corralitos, California (about 15 miles south of Santa Cruz) and shot her to death.

"Cynthia Schall was the next one. That happened the night I bought a .22 Rugar automatic pistol with a six inch barrel. And that night I killed her. Not so much to celebrate, but I was eagerly awaiting that gun," Kemper stated.

Victim, Cynthia (Cindy) Schall

After killing Schall, he took her body home and hid it in his bedroom closet. The next day while his mother was at work, he raped her corpse and dissected it in the bathtub with an electric saw.

Cynthia Ann Schall

Cynthia Ann Schall, circa 1971

He spread her body parts all over the county, but kept her head and buried it outside his bedroom window, where he would talk to it. "Sometimes at night, I'd talk to her, saying love things, the way you do to a girlfriend or wife." He made her head face upwards and joked that his mother always wanted someone to look up to her.

"Seven days later, a badly mutilated human torso was found floating in a lagoon near Santa Cruz. Two days after that, a surfer at Capitola found a left hand. And three days beyond that, someone else found a young woman's pelvis along the shore near Santa Cruz. Pieced together like a macabre jigsaw puzzle, this was the body of Cynthia Ann Schall." -truecrime.net

Edmund Kemper, the Co-Ed Killer of Santa Cruz

Body Is Identified -SC Girl

The sliced portions of a human body which have drifted into shore during the last week have been positively identified' by the coroner's office.

The victim has been named as Cynthia Ann Schall, 19, 220 Cleveland Ave. She had been reported missing Jan. 9, one day after she reportedly hitchhiked to a class at Cabrillo College.

It has not been determined by authorities whether the severed arms and legs found in Monterey County belong to Miss Schall. A corner's spokesman said that a meeting between local authorities and Monterey County officials will be held Thursday in an attempt to see if there is a connection.

Santa Cruz Sentinel, January 24, 1973

> *"If I killed them, you know, they couldn't reject me as a man. It was more or less making a doll out of a human being . . . and carrying out my fantasies with a doll, a living human doll."*
>
> -Ed Kemper

Kemper continued to hang out with the local cops at the Jury Room bar in Santa Cruz throughout his killing spree. He often spoke with them about the latest killings in the area, and even gave them his input at times. They had absolutely no idea the evil man they were relentlessly searching for was right in front of them.

On February 5th, 1973 (about a month after he murdered Schall) Kemper got in a fight with his mother and went out looking for someone to kill. "My mother and I had had a real tiff. I was pissed. I told her I was going to a movie and I jumped up and went straight to the campus because it was still early. I said, 'the first girl that's halfway decent that I pick up, I'm gonna blow her brains out.'"

At the Santa Cruz University, a little after 9 PM, Kemper picked up 23-year-old Rosalind Thorpe who was standing at the bus stop, hoping she hadn't missed the last bus. Kemper pulled up alongside Thorpe, rolled down his window and said, "The bus is gone. I know. I've missed it before, too. Can I give you a lift? It's pretty late." Rosalind got in the car and they drove off.

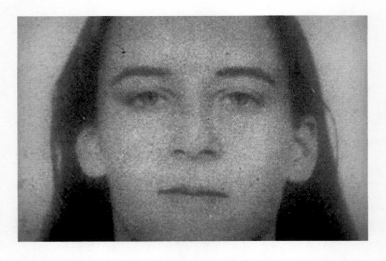

Rosalind Thorpe, victim of Ed Kemper

After driving a couple blocks, he picked up another UCSC student, 21-year-old Alice Helen (Allison) Liu, who was also hitchhiking.

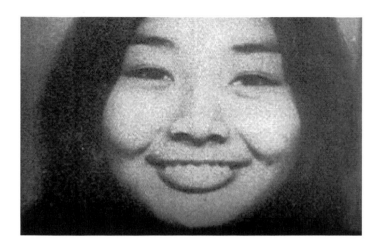

Alice Helen (Allison) Liu, victim of Ed Kemper

"Miss Liu was sitting in back right behind Miss Thorpe. I went on down a ways and slowed down. I remarked on the beautiful view. I hesitated for several seconds. I had been moving my pistol from down below my leg in my lap. I picked it up and pulled the trigger. As I fired, she fell against the window. Miss Liu panicked. I had to fire through her hands. She was moving around and I missed twice," Kemper stated.

He hit her in the temple, and then he aimed again and fired. After his two victims were dead, he wrapped them in blankets and proceeded to leave campus.

Two young men were at the campus security gate, but when they saw Kemper's university sticker they waved him through without any hesitation.

He took the girls' lifeless bodies home, where he decapitated them in his car that was parked in his mother's driveway. Afterward, he brought the girls' heads in his room to perform sexual acts on them.

"Ten days later, an Alameda County road crew was out checking for storm damage in the Eden Canyon area of the county north of Santa Cruz. Alongside a lonely road, up in a steep ravine, they made a horrifying discovery. At first, at a distance, they thought that what they had come upon were discarded mannequins. Up close, it was apparent that they were two mutilated corpses. Both women appeared to have been young, though the men were not certain. The bodies were headless. One seemed to be Asian and also had had her hands hacked off. She was nude. The white woman was clad in bra and panties." Hugh Stephens -Inside Detective Magazine, 1973.

A couple weeks later, their heads were found in San Mateo County.

ROSALIND THORPE AND ALICE LIU (RIGHT)
. . . identified as decapitated coeds
(Pensacola News-AP Wirephoto)

2 Decapitated

"With a girl, there's a lot left in the girl's body without a head. Of course the personality is gone."

-Ed Kemper

Side Note:

-      On February 13th, 1973, about a week after
the UCSC co-eds were killed and reported
missing, the other Santa Cruz serial killer,
Herbert Mullin was caught and arrested.

As the months went on, Kemper began to have
urges to kill more frequently. He was concerned
that his mother would find out what he had done,
so he decided that she would have to be killed
too.

A couple months later on April 21, 1973,
the 24-year-old serial killer decided it was
time for his mother to die. "I laid there in
bed thinking about it. And it's something hard
to just up and do. It was the most insane of
reasons for going and killing your mother. But
I was pretty fixed on that issue because there
were a lot of things involved. Someone just
standing off to the side, watching, isn't
really going to see any kind of sense, or rhyme,
or reason. -I had done some things, and felt
that I had to carry the full weight of

everything that happened. I certainly wanted for my mother a nice, quiet, easy death like I guess everyone wants," Kemper stated.

At 5:15 AM, he walked into his mother's room with a hammer in one hand and his knife in the other. Finding her sound asleep, Kemper hit his mother in her right temple with the hammer. She lay still with blood gushing from her head, still breathing, so her son flipped her onto her back and slit her throat with his knife.

Kemper thought to himself, "What's good for my victims is good for my mother," and decapitated her. He cut off his mother's left hand and then pulled out her larynx, stuffing it down the garbage disposal. The disposal clogged and regurgitated back up into the sink. "That seemed appropriate," Ed said after his arrest, "as much as she'd bitched, and screamed, and yelled at me over so many years." Kemper dragged his mother's lifeless body into a closet, and finished the deed by flipping over her blood-soaked bed mattress.

"It was so hard, I cut off her head, and I humiliated her, of course. She was dead, because of the way she raised her son," Ed shared.

After having sex with her severed head, he put it on the mantel and said what he wanted to say; and for the first time, she did not argue, which satisfied him. After speaking his mind, he threw darts at her head as it sat there staring blankly back at him.

After brutally murdering his 52-year-old mother, he knew he would undoubtedly be linked to this crime, so he decided he'd have to kill one of her friends to help deflect attention from him.

That afternoon, he called his mother's friend and co-worker, Sally (Sara) Hallett. He invited her to come over for dinner and a movie with him and his mother that evening. She arrived at the residence a little before eight o'clock wondering where Clarnell was. Edmund reassured her that his mother was just running late and would be home shortly. Sally said, "Let's sit down, I'm dead." "And I kind of took her on her word there," he said. Seeing that as his cue, he hit her in the stomach. She jumped back and yelled, "Guy! Stop that!" He struck her again and put her in a choke hold, strangling the 59-year-old woman to death.

Sally (Sara) Hallett, Kemper's final victim

After unclothing his final victim and laying her body on his bed, he satisfied his necrophilia once again.

Afterward, he drove Sally Hallett's car to the Jury Room Bar and parked it between two law officials' vehicles. He drank, smoked, and kept to himself that night; he seemed "standoffish," according to the patrons that had seen him that night.

At about midnight he went back to the murder scene and found Hallett's body was already in a state of rigor mortis, so he severed her head and had sex with it instead.

Then next morning he decided to get out of dodge before it was too late. He took the victims' credit cards and cash, and left a note in the house that read:

"No need for her to suffer anymore at the hands of this horrible 'murderous butcher.' It was quick, sleep, the way I wanted it."

He got in Sally's car and headed east. He drove straight to Reno, Nevada, where he ditched her car and rented another. He took a bunch of No-Doz and washed them down with soda, continuing to drive for eighteen hours straight.

Soon after he got to Colorado he was pulled over for speeding, was ticketed and let go.

Afraid that someone had discovered the bodies at his Aptos home, and that the FBI may be after him, he kept driving east for several more hours until he couldn't drive any longer. "It was very late at night. I was exhausted. And I was past exhaustion. I was just running on pure adrenaline. My body was quivering at times and my mind was slowing just beginning to unravel. I felt I was losing control, and I was afraid that anything could cause me to go off the deep end, and I didn't know what would happen then. I had never been out of control in my life … I finally had a thought. I was trying to think, 'Wow, I have got to stop this because it is getting so far out of hand. I am not going to be responsible for what happens any further. It is just going to happen,' and I didn't know what it was, and I didn't like that idea," Kemper stated.

Driving through the small town of Molly, Colorado, Edmund decided to pull over to a payphone and call the Santa Cruz Sherriff's office to confess and turn himself in.

He was arrested at the phone booth by Colorado police, and taken back to the old Santa Cruz County Jail in California.

SANTA CRUZ, Calif. (UPI) — A hulking young man who killed his grandparents nine years ago has confessed to eight recent slayings in the Santa Cruz area, including the hammer beating death of his mother.

Edmund Kemper, 24, a 6-foot-9 laborer, called authorities in Santa Cruz—the "murder capital of the world" —Tuesday from Pueblo, Colo., where he was arrested while still talking in the phone booth.

Daily Independent Journal, April 25, 1973

When the police arrived at the horrific crime scene, they found his mother and her friend's nude, beheaded bodies in the closets of the home.

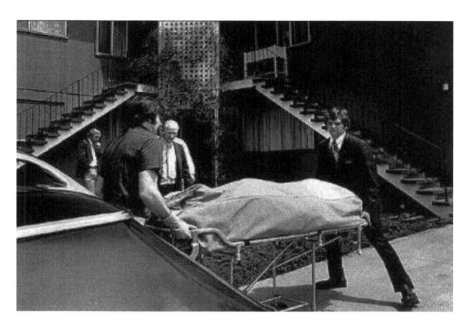

Crime Scene photo at the Kemper residence,
Aptos, CA, April 21, 1973

2 Women Slain In Aptos Home; Son Of One Held

Santa Cruz Sentinel, April 24, 1973

AP wirephotos

Clarnell Strandberg
. . . murdered

The San Bernardino County, April 26, 1973

The deranged killer cooperated with law enforcement during the arrest, and throughout the entire trial. Kemper lead investigators to all the body parts of his victims that he buried in and around the county.

An investigator pointing out where the head of one of Kemper's victims was buried at his former residence, Aptos, CA, 1973

Head Found In Aptos

Santa Cruz Sentinel, April 26, 1973

coed killer

Kemper's "souvenirs" from his helpless co-ed
victims, found at his former Aptos residence

"I had thought of annihilating the entire
block that I lived on."

-Ed Kemper

Kemper assisting investigators with locating remains of his victims, Santa Cruz mountains, 1973

Kemper at the Santa Cruz County Court House, 1973

> The defendant said on the witness stand he killed the women because "that was the only way they could be mine. I had their spirits. I still have them."

Dixon Evening Telegraph, November 9, 1973

His desire to possess the co-eds led Kemper even further than murder, he revealed in court. In his fantasies he literally made two of the girls "a part of me" by cooking and eating parts of them.

> The evidence presented in the Edmund Kemper murder trial shows that the matter is "the most enormous cold - blooded murder case in history," Santa Cruz Dist. Atty. Peter Chang said today in his final argument.
>
> Defense attorney Jim Jackson made no attempt during his closing statement to dispute the fact that Kemper killed eight women, including his mother, and said, "I do not suggest that he be able to walk the streets again."

Santa Cruz Sentinel, November 7, 1973

On November 8, 1973, the jury convened for five hours before declaring Kemper sane and guilty on all counts.

He asked for the death penalty, requesting "death by torture." Instead, he was sentenced to seven years to life for each count (8 total) at the California Medical Facility in Vacaville, California.

While being interviewed for a television show in prison, Kemper stated, "There's somebody out there that is watching this and hasn't done that - hasn't killed people, and wants to, and rages inside and struggles with that feeling, or is so sure they have it under control. They need to talk to somebody about it. Trust somebody enough to sit down and talk about something that isn't a crime; thinking that way isn't a crime. Doing it isn't just a crime, it's a horrible thing. It doesn't know when to quit and it can't be stopped easily once it starts."

"For over 40 years, Kemper's relatives have been living in fear that one of America's most notorious serial killers might be released from prison and come after them. Speaking publicly for the first time, David Weber - a name he uses to protect his identity - tells DailyMail.com: 'He has this control over the family, and there's still anger over what he did. So many people live in fear that he could be allowed freedom, you just can't trust what a President may decide.'" - Daily Mail.com

"I had fantasies about mass murder, whole groups of select women I could get together in one place, get them dead and then make mad, passionate love to their dead corpses. Taking life away from them, a living human being, and then having possession of everything that used to be theirs. All that would be mine. Everything."

-Ed Kemper

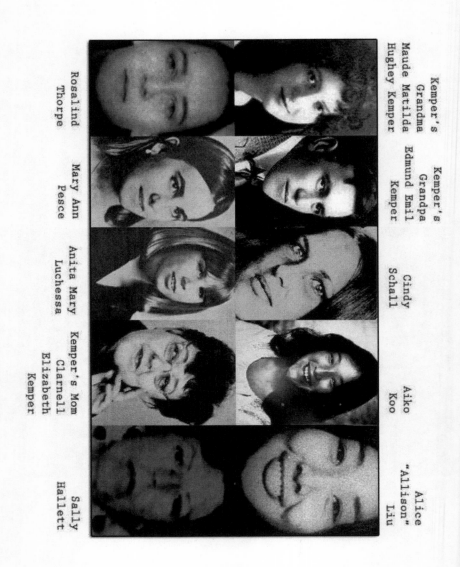

Ed Kemper's 10 victims

Edmund Kemper's Victims

- Maude Matilda Kemper, 66. August 27, 1964
- Edmund Emil Kemper, 72. August 27, 1964
- Mary Ann Pesce, 19. May 7, 1972
- Anita Mary Luccessa, 18. May 7, 1972
- Aiko Koo, 15. September 14, 1972
- Cynthia Ann (Cindy) Schall, 19. January 8, 1973
- Rosalind Thorpe, 23. February 5, 1973
- Alice (Allison) Liu, 21. February 5, 1973
- Clarnell Elizabeth Kemper (Strandberg), 52. April 21, 1973
- Sally (Sara) Hallett, 59. April 21, 1973

May you all rest in peace.

Terry Childs

Killer claims 11 more victims

APTOS, Calif. — A serial killer who said he is haunted in prison by the ghosts of his victims

Aptos murderer charged again

"Fill me up a fucken Uzi with about 60 clips ... I'd love to go out like that. Just stand up in the courtroom and tell Mr. D.A., ra-tat-tat-tat; the judge, ra-tat-tat-tat; the audience, ra-tat-tat-tat."

TERRY CHILDS

Santa Cruz Serial Killer

- <u>Date of birth</u>: 1955
- <u>Conviction(s)</u>: First-degree murder
- <u>Victims</u>: 12+
- <u>Span of killings</u>: June 11, 1974 - August 3, 1985
- <u>Date apprehended</u>: August 1985
- <u>Criminal penalty</u>: Life imprisonment
- <u>Former residence</u>: Aptos, California
- <u>Incarcerated at</u>: Salinas Valley State Prison, Soledad, California

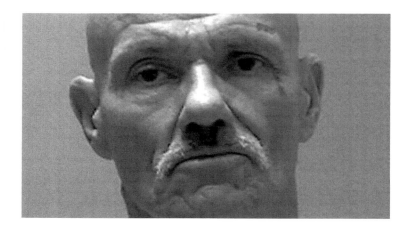

> ' If he told you that he killed somebody, yeah, you'd believe him too.'
>
> — *Christopher Smith, lawyer*

Santa Cruz Sentinel, July 19, 1997

The ill-famed serial killer from Aptos, California was convicted of murdering several people around the country; some investigators speculate that this psycho-killer slayed up to twenty-five people. In the 1970s and 1980s, Terry Childs killed five people in Santa Cruz, two of which he was convicted of murder.

A couple of his convictions happened as recently as 2016 when evidence was recently found by forensics.

Born in 1955, Childs grew up in Aptos, California. Deeply troubled from the start, he began having run-ins with the law when he was fifteen. His crimes escalated from robberies, and assaults with a deadly weapon, to rape, and brutal, unthinkable murders.

"Childs' rap sheet reads like a bad true-crime novel."

Terry Childs, the son of a bail bondsman, had studied police techniques to cover up his tracks while carrying out an unknown number of homicides.

Some of his siblings were also known to get into trouble with the law; one of his brothers was bludgeoned to death with a barbell in prison in the 90s.

On July 19, 1979, Terry Childs murdered Winnemucca school teacher Rulan McGill (32), in Sparks, Nevada. McGrill was on her way to a dentist appointment when she was captured, raped, and tragically murdered. Her nude body was found stabbed to death underneath some wooden pallets in a drainage ditch behind a Sparks' warehouse.

About four months later on November 6, 1979, nineteen-year-old Linda Ann Jozovich, from Aptos, California, who worked at a Mervyn's department store in Santa Clara, vanished during her dinner break. Childs had just gotten into a heated argument with his mother; exasperated, he began driving over the hill to Santa Clara, where he saw Jozovich walking across the parking lot. He then grabbed her and shoved her into his car. Terry Childs beat Linda Ann Jozovich and drove her up to the Santa Cruz Mountains where he strangled and stabbed the young vixen to death.

Terry Childs' victim, Linda Ann Jozovich

About fifteen years later a mushroom hunter found what was left of Jozovich's jawbone and a few of her ribs off of Black Road in the Santa Cruz Mountains.

Her death remained unsolved for over 28 years, until Childs confessed to her brutal murder in 2007, providing details to officials that had never been released to the public.

Then, on October 11th, 1984, twenty-eight-year-old New Jersey native Joan Leslie Mack was tragically raped and killed by Childs in Aptos, California. The homeless woman was found dead about a week later - bound and gagged with multiple stab wounds on the bluffs overlooking Seascape Beach in Aptos, California.

Joan Mack

Santa Cruz Sentinel, October 15, 1984

Terry Childs struck again on February 3rd, 1985. Santa Cruz resident Christopher Hall

(23) was found dead in a doorway on Dakota Street, near the entrance of San Lorenzo Park in Santa Cruz. He was slumped over in a pool of blood from a gunshot wound to his chest. It was unclear what Childs' motive was to kill Hall or if he even had one, some claim it was drug related as Childs was known to be a big meth and cocaine user.

On August 5th, 1985, 17-year-old Capitola resident Jeanine (Lois) Lynette Sigala's life was also taken at the hands of the psychotic killer. Lois found out Childs had stolen drugs from someone, so Terry decided to kill her for fear that she would snitch on him.

While Lois Sigala was sitting beneath a tree in a wooded area in Scotts Valley, California, Childs came toward her with a loaded 9mm and began shooting Lois in her arm and in her stomach, torturing her. As she began crawling to get away, screaming for her life, Childs shot her in the thigh to stop her from going any further. After shooting her 13 times, Terry's 14th and final shot was in her head. Her body was found near 2605 Granite Creek Road, Scotts Valley, California.

After Sigala's body had been found by police, a witness at the scene (Terry's girlfriend at the time) came forward and lead investigators to Terry's current address on Bennett Road in Aptos, California, where he was then arrested at thirty one years of age.

Childs' former home in Aptos, CA

Childs

Santa Cruz Serial Killer, Terry Childs

Terry Childs during trial, Santa Cruz, CA, 1985

Torture killing alleged

Santa Cruz Sentinel, January 21, 1987

In the 90s Terry Childs confessed to the murder of his father's fiancé, Penny Rickenbaker (30). Penny was shot in the head at her Aptos home at 309 Spreckels Drive, Aptos, CA, on June 11, 1974. When Penny's body was found by police in her bedroom, they speculated it was suicide, but said that they were going to investigate further. Due to lack of evidence, the case was closed, however, the family knew she wouldn't hurt nor kill herself, and that it was, in fact, foul play. They had a strong suspicion from the start that Terry Childs took his soon-to-be stepmother's life.

Aptos Woman Dies From Gun Wound

Santa Cruz Sentinel article, June 11, 1974

In March of 1987, on the day of Child's hearing at the Santa Cruz County Court House, he had planned for his dramatic exit to the world. Luckily, his hearing didn't go as he had planned.

"At the sentencing hearing, Chief Deputy District Attorney Robert Patterson played a tape recording a jailhouse conversation between Terry Childs and a woman friend, in which Childs told the woman he'd like her to bring him a loaded Uzi machine gun to court:

'Fill me up a fucken Uzi with about 60 clips … I'd love to go out like that. Just stand up in the courtroom and tell Mr. D.A., ra-tat-tat-tat; the judge, ra-tat-tat-tat; the audience, ra-tat-tat-tat.'

Childs told the woman to sit on one side of the courtroom, and he'd 'clean out' the other.

'Make my day,' Childs said. 'Let em plug me. Fuck it. Gotta run, it's been fun.'" - Santa Cruz Sentinel Article, March 5, 1987.

Charged with the four tragic homicides in Santa Cruz County (and convicted for two of them), Childs was charged for the murder of Rulan McGill in Sparks, Nevada. He was convicted with seven more murders around the country: two victims in Santa Clara, CA, one being Linda Ann Jozovich (19), two in Tracy, CA, one victim in San Diego, CA, and two victims in Seattle, WA.

Terry Childs was sentenced to life without parole. He is incarcerated at the Salinas Valley State Prison in Soledad, California.

Serial killer Terry Childs convicted of two new Santa Cruz County murders from 1980s

In 2016, Childs claimed to be haunted by the ghosts of some of his victims in his cell, staring at him, and "eating up his brain."-SF Gate, April 10, 2017

Aptos murderer charged again

New case supports convict's claim that he killed SV girl and 11 others

Santa Cruz Sentinel, November 8, 1997

Terry Child's (Known) Victims

- Penny Rickenbaker, 30.   June 11, 1974
- Rulan McGill, 32.   1979
- Linda Ann Jozovich, 19.   November 6, 1979
- Joan Lesley Mack, 28.   October 11, 1984
- Christopher Hall, 23.   February 3, 1985
- Jeanine Lois Sigala, 17.   August 5, 1985

Note: Childs was charged with seven more murders within the United States.

May you all rest in peace.

Other Killers

(who terrorized Santa Cruz)

DAVID JOSEPH CARPENTER

American Serial Killer

"The Trailside Killer"

- <u>Date of birth</u>: May 6, 1930
- <u>Conviction(s)</u>: Attempted murder, rape and attempted rape, kidnapping, robbery, murder
- <u>Victims</u>: 11+
- <u>Span of killings</u>: 1979-1981
- <u>Date apprehended</u>: May 15, 1981
- <u>Former residence</u>: San Francisco, CA
- <u>Criminal penalty</u>: Currently on death row
- <u>Incarcerated at</u>: San Quentin State Prison, San Quentin, California

Serial killer, David Carpenter during trial, 1981

Born in 1930 to abusive parents, David Joseph Carpenter spent most of his childhood in San Francisco's Glen Park district. His controlling mother made him take ballet when he was young and his peers teased and bullied him at school for it; he was also teased for playing the violin, and for his severe stutter. Carpenter resented his mother and women in general for the continued bullying. His "hellish" childhood was the root of his madness

138

and the monster that began to grow inside of him. He began torturing and killing animals as an outlet for his inner turmoil.

When Carpenter was fourteen he was committed to the Napa State Hospital for ninety days, after he molested two of his cousins, ages eight and three. He had discovered that during the molestation he felt completely in control and his stutter went away; this gave him confidence and heightened his urge to commit more violent and horrendous acts.

In the mid 1950s, David Carpenter joined the U.S. Coast Guard and eventually landed a job with Pacific Far East Lines as a purser. Soon after he began his job there, he met a woman named Ellen whom he married in 1955. They settled down in the seaside town of Pacifica, just south of San Francisco, where they had three children. In the beginning, things seemed to be pretty stable, but eventually David's anger resurfaced and the tension grew. He became very sexually demanding and prone to enraged outbursts.

Then, in 1960, when Carpenter was thirty years old, he took a turn for the worst. While giving a ride to acquaintance Lois Rinna, he came on to her, and when she refused, he hit her in the head multiple times with a hammer and proceeded to stab her in the hand with a knife. Luckily, an officer who happened to be patrolling the area at the time heard Rinna screaming, rescued her, and saved her life.

In 1961, David Carpenter was sentenced to fourteen years at McNeil Island Prison in Washington for the attempted murder of Lois Rinna.

His wife Ellen then filed for divorce.

In 1969, just eight years after attempting to brutally murder Lois Rinna, Carpenter was released from prison.

Shortly after he was released from prison, Carpenter met a woman named Helen in group therapy and the two married quickly after. It didn't take long for his second wife to figure out what kind of monster she had married.

In January of 1969, Helen took a vacation from Carpenter and his sexual needs. While she was away, he began to feel as if he was unable to control his compulsive sexual proclivities. He headed toward Boulder Creek, California in the Santa Cruz Mountains, where he had spent summers as a child at his grandparent's home. Familiar with the area, David drove around looking for a way to commit heinous deeds without returning to prison; he was prepared to eliminate witnesses.

While driving down Highway 9, near Boulder Creek, he got behind Cheryl Smith, a 19-year-old local woman. Carpenter purposely hit the back of her car so she would have to pull over and get out. As she stepped out of her vehicle, David grabbed her and forced her to climb up the nearby hillside. He began tearing off her clothes, and as she tried to get away he began stabbing her arms and leg. Smith managed to trick Carpenter into getting back into their cars by telling him that she would take him with her to her house to get bandages for her wounds. Instead, she drove into town, frightening David, so he fled.

Smith was able to give police both the description of David Carpenter and of his car, as well as his license plate number.

The very next day on January 28, 1970, Carpenter went after another helpless victim who lived up Empire Grade in Bonny Doon (also located in the Santa Cruz Mountains). He broke into a school teacher's home and awaited her arrival. When she and her children got home from school, David forced her to lie on the floor and tied her hands behind her back. As the children huddled in one of the bedrooms, Carpenter made the 35-year-old woman get into her car and he drove them to an abandoned cabin nearby where he raped her and eventually released her, stealing her car.

He headed north where he held another woman at gun point, raped yet another woman, and stole another car.

Carpenter was found and arrested a few months later and was charged with two counts of rape, one count of armed robbery, one count of burglary, and one count of kidnapping. He pleaded guilty to two of the charges, went to prison, and somehow was back on the streets just nine years later.

While in prison, some inmates claimed that David Carpenter told them he was in fact the notorious Zodiac Killer. Although he wasn't the Zodiac, it wasn't long before he was claiming multiple lives of his own.

On August 19, 1979, just three months after he had been released from prison, the forty-nine-year-old raped and shot his first murder victim. Forty-four-year-old Edda Kane was found dead and unclothed off the Rock Springs Trail in Mt. Tamalpais State Park, located in the San Francisco Bay area.

Carpenter returned to the park on March 8, 1980, where he raped and stabbed to death local resident Barbara Schwartz (23), who had been walking alone with her dog.

On October 11, 1980, Richard Stowers (19) of Petaluma, and Cynthia Moreland (18) of Cotati were shot and killed in Point Reyes National Park (Seashore), located in Marin County near San Francisco, California.

On October 15, 1980, Anne Alderson (26) of San Rafael was found dead near Mt. Tamalpais Park. She had been sexually assaulted and shot three times.

A few weeks later, the "Trailside Killer" took two more lives on November 28, 1980 in Point Reyes National Park Seashore. The bodies of Diane O'Connell (22) of San Jose, and Shauna May (25) of San Francisco were found in shallow graves after being raped and shot to death.

Not far from the two bodies, laid Richard Stowers and Cynthia Moreland who had been missing since their deaths.

Five of the victims had been on their knees when they were shot in the back head with the same murder weapon, a .38-caliber Rossi revolver.

On June 16, 1981, the remains of Carpenter's acquaintance Anna Kelly Menjivar (17) were found in Castle Rock State Park, located in the Santa Cruz and Los Gatos Mountains. How she was murdered is unknown, for there were very little remains when she was found six months later. The Daly City girl

disappeared December 28, 1980, and was believed
to have been a runaway, until her parents saw
Carpenter on the news, and notified authorities
that Anna knew him. Miss Menjivar was a part-
time teller in San Francisco at the bank where
Carpenter had an account. Her parents said
that David had even given her a couple rides in
the past, and that he seemed to be a nice man.

On March 29, 1981 two 20-year-old UC Davis
students were hiking in Henry Cowell Redwood
State Park, located in the Santa Cruz
Mountains. As Ellen Marie Hansen and her friend
Steven Haertle were walking along the Ridge
Trail, Carpenter approached them. Pointing his
gun at the hikers, he told Haertle to leave so
he could rape Hansen. Steven began begging
David to let them go, telling him they wouldn't
say anything if he released them. Carpenter
continued to tell Haertle to go down the trail
so he could sexually assault Hansen. Hansen
then very bravely said out loud, "Don't listen
to him, Steve, because he's going to shoot us
anyway." Haertle refused to leave and seconds
later the Trailside Killer pointed the gun at
Hansen and shot her in the head. He then shot

145

Haertle three times. "I remember falling to the ground with a buzzing sensation in my arm and everything was slowing down. I was laying on the ground next to Ellen. I picked up Ellen's head and saw that she was bleeding; and then I look up to see the suspect with his back turned to me. I began running up the trail as fast as I could," Heartle said. He saw two hikers who helped him to an observation deck. Steven had gotten away, but not before Carpenter passed them; both witnesses got a good look at him. "That's the man who shot me! Run!!" Heartle exclaimed. The killer, of course, made a run for it and vanished. Ellen died from her wound later that day.

Carpenter's victim, Ellen Hansen

Steven gave a detailed description of the suspect to the police who released a sketch of the killer.

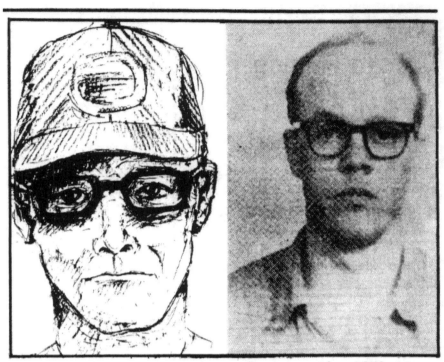

Police Sketch Of Suspect   **Carpenter After 1970 Arrest**

Santa Cruz Sentinel, May 15, 1981

The sketch above was circulated around California, and within five days, an anonymous Ben Lomond woman gave the name David Joseph Carpenter to the police.

On May 2, 1981, Carpenter offered to take a co-worker of his to check out a car that was for sale in Santa Cruz. Twenty-year-old Heather Scaggs from San Jose, California worked with Carpenter at the California Trade School in Hayward.

Carpenter's victim, Heather Scaggs

Leery of David, Heather went anyway, but she let her housemates know where she was going ahead of time, and even told them that if she didn't return that night to call the police. Unfortunately, her instincts were spot on; her

148

body was found a few weeks later in Big Basin Park located in Boulder Creek, California.

Two hikers had found Scaggs slightly covered in leaves and brush about 150 yards from Upper China Grade Road inside the state park. She had been raped and shot to death.

Carpenter sold his revolver to a friend soon after his last murder, who in the end, handed the gun over to authorities, testifying that she bought it from the Trailside Killer.

On May 15, 1981, David Carpenter was arrested for the murders of Ellen Hansen and Heather Scaggs by Santa Cruz police at his parent's house, (whom he had been living with again) located at 38 Sussex Street, in Glen Park, California.

On May 10, 1988, a San Diego jury convicted Carpenter on five counts of first-degree murder for the slayings of Diane O'Connell, Anne Alderson, Richard Stowers, Cynthia Moreland, and Shauna May. Carpenter was also found guilty of raping two of the women.

Following his conviction for the Marin County murders, Carpenter was tried and convicted by a Santa Cruz jury for the murders and attempted rape of Ellen Hansen and Heather Scaggs, and for the attempted murder of Steven Haertle.

Jim Berglund, Santa Cruz County assistant district attorney who with District Attorney Art Danner prosecuted the case, said Thursday that Carpenter is "without a doubt the most evil, self-serving and manipulative person I've ever encountered in this line of work. He humiliated his victims before shooting them at point-blank range, and he's absolutley without remorse for any of the crimes he's committed.

"He's a rapist who's learned to kill his victims and likes to kill his victims."

Santa Cruz Sentinel, November 16, 1984

David Carpenter
'Trailside Killer'

Jury urges gas chamber for hiking trail killer

LOS ANGELES (AP) — A jury on Friday urged a judge to sentence convicted "Trailside Killer" David Carpenter to death in the gas chamber for the murders of two women on hiking trails among California's redwood trees.

Carpenter, 54, was convicted by another jury last July of murdering Ellen Marie Hansen and Heather Scaggs, both 20, in separate 1981 attacks in Santa Cruz County and of attempted murder on Hansen's companion, Steven Haertle, then 20.

St. Cloud Times, October 26, 1984

In 1984, the Trailside Killer was sentenced to die in the gas chamber.

As of now (2020), Carpenter (89) remains on death row at San Quentin, still claiming that he's innocent.

In 1995, the Santa Cruz convictions were overturned due to juror misconduct. The California Supreme Court later reinstated the Santa Cruz convictions.

In December of 2009, police re-examined evidence from the 1979 murder of twenty-three-year-old Mary Frances Bennett, who was jogging at Lands End in San Francisco, California, when she was attacked and brutally stabbed two dozen times. A DNA sample obtained from the scene was matched to David Carpenter through state Department of Justice files. Prosecutors have not yet decided whether to file charges based on the new evidence.

David Carpenter's Victims

- Edda Kane, 44. August 19, 1979
- Mary F. Bennett, 23. October 21, 1979
- Barbara Schwartz, 23. March 8, 1980
- Richard Stowers, 19. October 11, 1980
- Cynthia Moreland, 18. October 11, 1980
- Anne Alderson, 26. October 15, 1980
- Diane O'Connell, 22. November 28, 1980
- Shauna May, 25. November 28, 1980
- Anna Kelly Menjivar, 17. December 28, 1980
- Ellen Marie Hansen, 20. March 29, 1981
- Heather Scaggs, 20. May 2, 1981

May you all rest in peace.

WILLIAM "BILLY" MANSFIELD JR.

Serial Killer, Rapist

- <u>Date of birth</u>: 1956
- <u>Conviction(s)</u>: Rape, first-degree murder
- <u>Victims</u>: 5+
- <u>Span of killings</u>: 1976-1980
- <u>Date apprehended</u>: 1980
- <u>Criminal penalty</u>: 25 years to life in prison
- <u>Former residence</u>: KOA Campground, San Andreas Road, Watsonville, CA
- <u>Incarcerated at</u>: California State Prison, Solano, CA

In 1980, twenty-five-year-old William "Billy" Mansfield Jr. from Weeki Wachee Acres, Florida, moved to Santa Cruz with his brother, Gary (23). They lived in a tent and a 12-foot trailer at the KOA Campground on San Andreas Road, in Watsonville, California.

Billy worked at Miranda Mushrooms, a farm between Watsonville and Monterey, where he had a reputation of being drunk on the job.

From a young age, Billy couldn't keep his hands to himself. He had a long history of molesting and raping women, and had just gotten out of jail for sexually assaulting two teenage girls. His father was also a convicted rapist and child molester.

Mansfield was known to frequent his neighborhood bar, The Wooden Nickel Too, where he'd pick up on women. One night on December 6th, 1980, while drinking at the bar, Billy met Rene Saling, a 29-year-old married mother of three, who was looking for her husband. Mansfield and Saling were seen together by multiple people that night, and it was the last time Rene was ever seen alive.

Billy Mansfield's victim, Rene Saling

The next morning, Saling's partially
clothed body was found in a drainage ditch near
the county dump on Buena Vista Drive in
Watsonville. A black cord was wound so tightly
around her neck that part of it disappeared
into her flesh.

Along with several witnesses seeing the two
together, a single thread from Saling's blouse
was found on a pair of Mansfield's pants that
laid in his van, linking him to the murder.

Billy's 23-year-old brother, Gary Mansfield, was also a suspect in the Saling case.

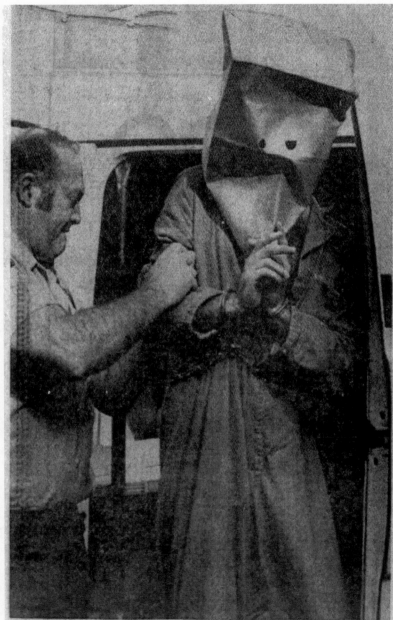

In December 23, 1980, Mansfield was headed for court in Watsonville, Calif., on the charge of murdering Rene Saling. He was dubbed the "grocery bag killer" because his lawyers wanted to protect his identity during court appearances.

While awaiting trial in Santa Cruz for the murder of Saling, Billy's parents' property in Florida was searched by police due to the disappearances of other young women. There, four bodies were uncovered; Billy had buried them separately on the property, indating back to 1975.

Billy was convicted of murder, and pleading guilty to strangling the four women to death. In 1982, he was sentenced to 25 years to life at the California State Prison Solano, in Vacaville, California.

He is also a suspect in two other homicides in Florida.

Mansfield guilty of slaying woman in Watsonville

San Francisco Examiner, February 24, 1982

"I have killed a lot of people, both males and females. I'm starting to have that feeling again, like I did before. Something inside me says, 'kill him.'"

-Billy Mansfield

Convicted murderer Billy Mansfield Jr. will be tried Sept. 7 for the Florida murders of four young women whose bodies were unearthed on his parents' junk-strewn property last year.

This week, prosecutors and detectives from Florida paid a visit to Santa Cruz. They were seeking evidence which could be used in their trial.

Florida Deputy State Attorney Jimmy Brown will be trying the case against Mansfield. He said he expects the trial to last about a month.

The trial has been moved from Hernando County, where Mansfield is currently housed, and will be held in Panama City, on the Florida panhandle.

Mansfield, 26, was convicted by a Marin County jury in February of the murder of Watsonville housewife Rene Saling, 29. She was strangled Dec. 7 with a black cord.

Investigators say one of the victims in Florida was found with a similar cord around her neck. They hope to use Mansfield's conviction for the Saling murder as evidence to prove a similar criminal pattern with the Florida cases.

Two of the dead women whose bodies were found in Florida have not been identified, but investigators say they are still pursuing leads.

The other two victims have been identified as being Sandra Jean Graham, who disappeared from a Tampa lounge in April, 1980, and Elaine Ziegler, a 15-year-old girl who was staying at a KOA campground near the Mansfield home. She was last seen with a man fitting Mansfield's description on New Year's Eve, 1975, investigators said.

If convicted of the Florida murders, Mansfield could receive the death penalty.

RICHARD ANTHONY SOMMERHALDER

Killer, Rapist

- <u>Date of birth</u>: January 3, 1947
- <u>Date of death</u>: May 12, 1994 (aged 47 years)
- <u>Place of death</u>: Texoma Medical Center, Denison, Oklahoma
- <u>Cause of death</u>: Cancer
- <u>Conviction(s)</u>: Robbery, rape, second-degree murder
- <u>Murder Victims</u>: 3+
- <u>Span of killings</u>: 1976
- <u>Date apprehended</u>: 1976
- <u>Criminal penalty</u>: nine years in prison, parole

On June 26, 1976, Santa Cruz residents Mary Gorman (21), and Vicki Bezore (31) went on a drive and never returned. Gorman's car was found the following day in the mountains with blood covering the front and back seats.

Eight weeks later the victims' badly decomposed, naked bodies were found by hikers in the redwood grove, near the Henry Cowell State Park entrance off Highway 9, in Felton, California. Along with being kidnapped and raped, Vicki Bezore was badly beaten to death, and Mary Gorman was both beaten and stabbed.

Mary Gorman   **Vicki Bezore**

Santa Cruz Sentinel, August 12, 1976

A sheriff's investigation van marks the spot off Highway 9 where the decomposed bodies of two women were discovered Wednesday. The bodies were located some 184 feet from the roadside in a heavily wooded area. They were discovered by two hikers looking for firewood in the area.

Bodies Of 2 Women Found

Santa Cruz Sentinel, August 12, 1976

District Attorney Chris Cottle said that testimonies from various witnesses and a couple "breaks" in the case lead them to the arrest of 29-year-old Richard "Blue" Sommerhalder from Aptos, who had just been charged with raping two young local women in Rio Del Mar months prior.

Aptos Man Held For Killing 2 Women

Santa Cruz Sentinel, September 1, 1976

Sommerhalder had just moved to Santa Cruz a year prior and opened a tiny novelty head shop in Rio Del Mar, where he sold homemade pipes, as well as cocaine out of the register.

In his younger years, Blue was part of a motorcycle gang called the Grim Reapers, whose motto was, "Ride, rob, rape, and kill." His older brother was a former president of the greatly-feared biker gang from Santa Rosa, California, before going to prison for first degree murder.

Surprisingly, Blue's mother claimed he was a "happy child" despite the family having constant financial problems.

The Nazi was convicted of second-degree murder for the slayings of Gorman and Bezore, and was sentenced to nine years at Soledad Prison, in Soledad, California.

He was also a main suspect in the murder of 26-year-old Karen Percifield, whose body was found in a brushy Aptos ravine on May 28, 1976. She had been stabbed twice in the chest. Visiting from Ohio, Percifield had been last seen at the Bay View Hotel in Aptos with her sister and mother, before getting into a heated argument with them and leaving.

'Murder capital' stirs again

The Press Democrat, August 13, 1976

In 1986, when being released, he asked to be paroled to Santa Cruz, but the county declined after residents argued vehemently against his return. He was then sent to another state, where he threatened to kill his parole officer.

SC killer can't escape past

Santa Cruz Sentinel, February 20, 1990

In 1994, Sommerhalder died of cancer at forty-seven years of age at the Texoma Medical Center, in Denison, Oklahoma.

WILLIAM ROGERS

Mass Murderer

- <u>Date of birth</u>: 1939
- <u>Date of death</u>: July 6, 1980 (aged 41)
- <u>Place of death</u>: 305 Riverview Avenue, Capitola, California
- <u>Cause of death</u>: Suicide
- <u>Victims</u>: 5 (including himself)
- <u>Date of mass murder</u>: July 6, 1980

Suicide-Murders Leave Five Dead

Santa Cruz Sentinel, July 7, 1980

It was an early Sunday morning, around 5 AM, on July 6, 1980, when several screams and gun shots were heard throughout the Capitola Village in Santa Cruz County. Forty-one-year-old William Rogers from Redding, California was the cause of the horrific event that took five lives, including his own. Soon after his wife, Christine Rogers (39) took their three daughters to stay with her parents overlooking the Soquel Creek, William arrived to confront her. Rogers kicked in the door located at 305 Riverview Avenue, Capitola, which strangely and coincidentally was also the same residence in which another murder had occurred in 1972.

As Rogers began kicking down the door, Joan, their fifteen-year-old daughter, was calling the police. While speaking with dispatch, Rogers entered the home holding a 12-

guage shotgun, telling his wife that "if they didn't get back together again, he was going to kill everybody."

The dispatcher heard the sounds of the gun fire and Joan screaming.

"Then everyone started screaming. At one point, the girl screamed and dropped the phone. Seconds later there was a loud scream, and then a shot -- the sound of the teenager being killed. Then there was silence for about 40 seconds, and the sound of the shot that took William Rodgers' life."

When officers arrived, they found only the bodies of the family. "It was horrible," said Detective Herb Ross.

Mrs. Rodgers' body was found lying in the kitchen with the body of her seventeen-year-old daughter at her feet.

One of the girls was lying on a pull-out bed, and another was slumped over an end table.

Mr. Rodgers' body was found lying in the hallway of the one bedroom home.

Christine's parents managed to get away unharmed.

The Rogers family was laid to rest at Santa Cruz Memorial, in Santa Cruz, California.

Man kills himself after slaying family

CAPITOLA, Calif. (AP) — A man who kicked his way into his in-laws' house in this resort town shot his estranged wife and three daughters to death and then killed himself, police said.

Green Bay Press Gazette July 7, 1980

At one point, the girl screamed and dropped the phone. Seconds later, there was a loud scream and then a shot — the sound of the teen-ager being killed.

Santa Cruz Sentinel, July 7, 1980

Author's Notes

This book wasn't easy to write; with the topic being so tragic, sick, and quite nauseating ... it took a while. But it's a part of Santa Cruz history, and I felt it was something that needed to be researched and written about. So, here it is.

Please know this book was written for educational and informational purposes, and is not in any way written to offend.

My heart goes out to all the victims and their loved ones...

Sources

Books:

- Cheney, Margaret. <u>Why: The Serial Killer in America</u>. iUniverse.com Inc. Lincoln, NE, 2000

- Graysmith, Robert. <u>The Sleeping Lady</u>. Penguin Books, New York, 1990

- Lunde, Donald T. and Morgan, Jefferson. <u>The Die Song</u>. WW Norton and Company, New York, 1980

- Swinney, C.L. <u>Deadly Voices</u>. RJ Parker Publishing, Inc. USA, 2015

- Whittington-Egan, Richard. <u>Murder on File</u>. Neil Wilson Publishing, 2011

Articles:

- Anonymous. "Inmate to Undergo Tests on Claim of 12 Killings." New York Times, July 21, 1997

- Anonymous. "Kemper's Young Fiancé in Shock." Greeley Daily Tribune, May 5, 1973

- Anonymous. "Limbs Belong to Body." Santa Cruz Sentinel, January 26, 1973

- Anonymous. "Body is identified. -SC Girl." Santa Cruz Sentinel, January 24, 1973

- Anonymous. "Santa Cruz Murder Victims Wanted to Live in the Wilds." Independent Journal, February 19, 1973

- Anonymous. "Kemper Declared 'Harmless' Two Days After Girl Killed." Progress Bulletin, May 1, 1973

- Anonymous. "Local Girl Strangled." The Tustin News, November 29, 1979

- Anonymous. "Jury Urges Gas Chamber for Hiking Trail Killer." St. Cloud Times, October 6, 1984

- Anonymous. "Henry Cowell Park: Blossoms and Bodies." Santa Cruz Sentinel, April 26, 1984

- Anonymous. "Suicide Murders Leave Five Dead." Santa Cruz Sentinel, July 7, 1980

- Anonymous. "Murder Capital Stirs Again." The Press Democrat, August 13, 1976

- Anonymous. "Trailside Killer was spotted by FBI." Ukiah Journal, May 22, 1981

- Anonymous. "Death Penalty for Carpenter." Santa Cruz Sentinel, November 16, 1984

- Bergstrom, Mark. "Four More Counts Against Mullin." Santa Cruz Sentinel, February 20, 1973

- Honig, Tom. "5 Slain in Two Cases." Santa Cruz Sentinel, January 26, 1973

Serial Killers of Santa Cruz

- Honig, Tom. "Mullin Link to Slaying Priest." Santa Cruz Sentinel, February 16, 1973

- Honig, Tom. "Mullin is Found Guilty." Santa Cruz Sentinel, August 20, 1973

- Honig, Tom. "Kemper is charged with Six Counts of Murder." Santa Cruz Sentinel, April 26, 1973

- Honig, Tom. "Gruesome Details on Tape at Trial." Santa Cruz Sentinel, October 25, 1973

- Honig, Tom. "Jury Finds Kemper Guilty." Santa Cruz Sentinel, November 8, 1973

- Johnson, Cliff. "Lawmen Name Suspect in SLV Assault Cases." Santa Cruz Sentinel, January 30, 1970

- Larson, Amy. "Serial Killer Admits to Unsolved Murders in Aptos and Santa Cruz." SF Gate, April 10, 2017

- Palmer, Richard. "Killer of 13 Wants His Freedom." The Valley Press, July 1, 1981

- Townsend, Peggy. "Body Found; Carpenter Suspect." Santa Cruz Sentinel, May 26, 1981

- Townsend, Peggy. "The Killers Next Door." Santa Cruz Sentinel, March 13, 2005

- Townsend, Peggy. "UCSC Coed Found Slain in Cowell Park." Santa Cruz Sentinel, November 23, 1979

- York, Jessica. "Aptos Serial Killer Terry Childs Convicted of Two New Murders From 1980s." Santa Cruz Sentinel, April 10, 2017

Web:

- http://allthingscrimeblog.com/2014/01/16/when-santa-cruz-was-the-murder-capital-of-the-world-part-three-2/
- http://crimefeed.com/tag/terry-childs/
- http://criminalminds.wikia.com/
- http://murderpedia.org/male.C/c/carpenter-david-joseph.htm
- http://murderpedia.org/male.M/m/mullin-herbert.htm
- http://serialkillercalendar.com/edmundkemper.html
- http://truecrimecases.blogspot.com/2012/08/edmund-kemper.html
- http://www.criminalmotives.com/serial-killers/serial-killers/edmund-kemper/
- http://www.geocities.ws/narcolet/Herbert_Mullin_The_Terminator.html
- http://www.kion546.com/news/serial-killer-admits-slaying-slaying-2-in-aptos-and-santa-cruz/445888382
- http://www.sfgate.com/bayarea/article/Convicted-killer-charged-with-murder-in-South-Bay-3301733.php

- http://www.sfweekly.com/news/snitch/yesterdays-crimes/yesterdays-crimes-murder-prevents-earthquakes/
- http://www.sparselysageandtimely.com/blog/?p=6213
- http://www.zodiackillersite.com/viewtopic.php?t=1328&p=13816
- https://en.wikipedia.org/
- https://fresnoalliance.com/the-prison-press-conversation-with-david-carpenter-aka-the-trailside-killer/
- https://herbertwilliammullin.org/
- https://lasvegassun.com/news/1997/nov/05/convicted-killer-indicted-in-winnemucca-teachers-d/
- https://nypost.com/2016/02/10/serial-killer-quoted-in-american-psycho-doesnt-want-to-leave-jail/
- https://williamdukepresents.com/category/the-trailside-killer/
- https://williamdukepresents.com/tag/david-carpenter/
- https://www.bartleby.com/essay/Herbert-Mullins-a-Case-Study-of-a-P3AZ4Y4K6YYA
- https://www.biography.com/people/edmund-kemper-403254
- https://www.dailymail.co.uk/news/article-5168247/Brother-Edmund-Kempner-speaks-time.html
- https://www.mercurynews.com/2009/08/18/soquel-mass-murderer-john-linley-frazier-found-dead-in-prison/

- https://www.mistersf.com/notorious/index.html?not trailside02.htm
- https://www.psychologytoday.com/us/blog/wicked-deeds/201403/the-real-life-horror-tale-the-twisted-co-ed-killer
- https://www.santacruzpl.org/history/articles/116/
- https://patch.com/california/watsonville/man-convicted-of-brutally-murdering-woman-in-watsonvieac2a74f08

About the Author

Aubrey Graves studied criminal behavior and law at Cabrillo College in Aptos, California. She has always had an interest in the history of her hometown, Santa Cruz, the once alleged "Murder Capital of the World."

aubreygraves@hotmail.com

Made in the USA
Middletown, DE
05 September 2023

37593760R00106